# VULCANS
## EARTHLINGS
### and Marketing ROI

# VULCANS
# EARTHLINGS
## and Marketing ROI

### Getting Finance, Marketing and Advertising
### onto the Same Planet

David Rutherford and Jonathan Knowles

Wilfrid Laurier University Press

We acknowledge the financial support of the Government of Canada through the Book Publishing Industry Development Program for our publishing activities.

 Institute *of* Communication Agencies

Library and Archives Canada Cataloguing in Publication

Rutherford, David
  Vulcans, earthlings and marketing ROI : getting finance, marketing and advertising onto the same planet / David Rutherford and Jonathan Knowles.

Co-published by the Institute of Communication Agencies.
Includes bibliographical references and index.
ISBN 978-1-55458-031-6

  1. Marketing—Finance. 2. Advertising—Rate of return. 3. Brand name products—Valuation. 4. Rate of return. I. Knowles, Jonathan. II. Institute of Communication Agencies. III. Title.

HF5415.R87 2007                 658.8                 C2007-906928-2

# Contents

*Part 3. Creating a Shared Accountability Culture*

# Foreword from the ICA

Institute *of*
Communication Agencies

As you read this, a couple of twenty-somethings in a basement somewhere are inventing the next YouTube or Facebook—giving companies yet more ways to reach their audiences. With all this change, however, one thing is constant. Our clients still need to make sensible investments, and get a good return.

In the early 1990s, there were no Balanced Scorecards or Marketing Dashboards, but Rupert Brendon, our former President, wanted to make a statement about advertising's business effectiveness. The result was the Cassies show, running now for fifteen years. It is the only advertising award show based on the success of "sensible and prudent investment" as demonstrated by rigorous published cases.

In those days, the CEOs at the big advertisers often came out of Brand Management. They knew what marketing could do, *and* how hard it was to measure this with any precision. They used the available tools, but they also made a lot of decisions based on experience and judgment.

Nowadays, Accountability is the new watchword. But Rupert noticed something about the often impenetrable material on the topic. Authors reflected their particular world view, and nothing bridged the different ways that Finance, Marketing and Advertising look at business. That's when he enlisted David Rutherford and Jonathan Knowles, who between them are fluent in the three disciplines. They agreed to take on the challenge of writing a book for the ICA that:

- Reflects the Finance, Marketing and Advertising viewpoints.
- Is rigorous, while still being an easy read.

As the book says more than once, there's no quick fix. The answer is an Accountability Culture that values ideas, and builds profitable brands. Our members are determined to play their part in this, and we dedicate this book to proven and measurable success for our clients.

**Gillian Graham**
Chief Executive Officer
Institute of Communication Agencies
November 5, 2007

# Preface

Every few years, business is galvanized by a new concept. Strategic Planning, Positioning, Shareholder Value, Globalization, the Balanced Scorecard and many others have all seized the imagination.

Accountability is the latest idea in the spotlight. It's a huge topic, and in the broadest sense embraces ethics, corporate governance and all the issues spawned by the recent spate of business scandals.

This book deals with a more pragmatic aspect: the Accountability behind the question, "are our investments in marketing and advertising sensible and successful, short and long term, from a business point of view?"

As the cartoon suggests, this tempts some people to avoid the topic, and others to hope for a silver bullet. This book describes a more demanding (but ultimately more rewarding) approach.

Our central theme is the dissonance between the two world views observed in business. The first is the logic and reason world view of the Vulcan. It predominates in Finance, Operations, and the C-Suite. The second predominates with Marketing and Advertising people. They agree that the logical view is, well, logical. But they know from long experience that Earthling behaviour frequently defies simple logic and reflects a powerful combination of functional, emotional and social factors.

We believe that business needs to resolve this dissonance. Disturbingly, it isn't happening to any great extent at present. A recent report by the UK's Chartered Institute of Marketing noted that only 14% of the top 100 companies on the London Stock Exchange have a marketer at board level, and only 17% of CEOs have a marketing background.

This under-representation of the Earthling perspective will surely be detrimental to the long-term health of business. Hence the goal of this book:

**To get Finance, Marketing and Advertising onto the same planet—to the benefit of all concerned.**[*]

---

[*] We are using "Finance" in the broad sense. It includes Accounting, Budgeting, etc.

# Introduction

At a recent meeting the pressure to be proactive was so great that it was impossible to think. Suddenly someone said, "This started as a Ready-Aim-Fire meeting, right? But do we really need Ready?" This got a laugh. Then someone else chimed in, "Come to think of it, do we really need Aim?" More laughter. Then the alpha male topped everyone. "That's right. All we need [as he launched into all the theatrics of a machine gunner] is F-I-I-I-IRE!!"

We've seen Accountability generate this hair-trigger reaction. But a subject this important needs a more strategic approach. As a result, this book is in three parts.

In Part 1 we establish that Finance, Marketing and Advertising share common ground in the value of brands. P&G paid ten times book value for Gillette because of the ability of its brands to win the hearts and minds of consumers and (to use Finance terminology) create profit and growth at favourable risk.

Part 2 reviews the evidence for the business impact of marketing and advertising, summarizing key research and practical experience.

Part 3 then outlines what it takes to build an Accountability Culture and profiles some techniques that are useful for framing and measuring the business impact of marketing and advertising investment.

### Who This Book Is For

Our audience is anyone with an interest in Accountability, as it applies to short- and long-term marketing effort. In other words, we are addressing Finance, Marketing, and Advertising—and the related disciplines.

Within this, we have client and agency C-Suites especially in mind. This is because Vulcan-Earthling dissonance needs firm and diplomatic resolution from the top.*

---

\* We are using "agency" in the broad sense, to avoid the clumsiness of "marketing communication services provider."

### A New Mindset

Accountability can be achieved in a host of different ways, but there's a common thread—the right mindset. To establish this, we have three objectives:

- To convince Marketing and Advertising to talk to Finance in the language of Finance.
- To convince Finance to expand on their Vulcan world view.
- To consign to history the mutually unflattering stereotypes that Finance, Marketing and Advertising have of each other.

### English as She Is Spoke

This is the title of a 19th century Portuguese-English phrase book—hilariously off-base because its authors didn't speak English. We hope we've done better, in that one of us (DR) is fluent in Marketing and Advertising, and the other (JK) is fluent in Marketing and Finance.

As for language, most books and papers on our topic are very heavy going. We've decided to keep specialist terminology to a minimum.

There's a risk in this, of course, because some of the concepts we cover are complex—and it will not do them (or us) justice if they come across as simplistic. On the other hand, we don't want to send you to sleep, even if you are reading this on a plane!

Finally, there's an extensive—sometimes light hearted—glossary at the back of the book.

### Footnotes and References

To keep the narrative flowing, we've used footnotes extensively. They amplify key points, but you can skim over them if you so choose. A full list of references is at the back of the book.

### On the Shoulders of Giants

A number of people have had a profound influence on our thinking. We would like to single out for special acknowledgment:

David Aaker, and in particular his book *Brand Leadership*.

Tim Ambler, who wrote *Marketing and the Bottom Line*. It opens with the astonishing comment that boards of directors devote nine times more time to "spending and counting cash flow than wondering where it comes from and how it could be increased."

Leslie Butterfield, who edited and part-authored *AdValue*, detailing ways that advertising adds value to business.

Pat LaPointe and colleagues, who have written extensively on Accountability and ROI, publishing this at www.marketingnpv.com.

Alan Middleton, who wrote *Measuring Marketing Communication Returns—ROI or Dashboard?* for the Association of Canadian Advertisers.

Srivastava, Shervani and Fahey, who wrote "Building and Leveraging Market-Based Assets to Drive Marketplace Performance and Value." As an academic paper it can be forgiven its unwieldy title, but the message is clear. Strong brands, managed well, lead to better cash flow and higher stock prices.

Finally, PIMS (Profit Impact of Marketing Strategy). This is a huge database maintained by the Strategic Planning Institute, a non-profit corporation affiliated with Harvard University. It is a treasure trove of information and insight, and contains data on the marketing and financial performance of almost half the Fortune 1000.

## About the Authors

*David Rutherford*

David graduated in the UK as a Civil Engineer, and the theme of "constructing things that work" has continued throughout his career. He came to marketing via seven years at Procter & Gamble (Canada). There, he became the P&G equivalent of a Category Manager, with Tide—then P&G's biggest brand—in his portfolio. After he left P&G David joined Ogilvy & Mather Toronto, where he rose to become President, and later Vice Chairman. In 1991 David set up as a consultant, specializing in marketing, advertising, and business writing. David is also the long-standing Editor for the Cassies, the annual award show for advertising that proves business-building effectiveness via a rigorous written case. David has reviewed over 200 winning cases, publishing the lessons that "cross over" from one case to another. (Crossover Notes can be seen at www.cassies.ca.) David also wrote the ICA guide to Client-Agency Evaluation, and is Editor and contributing author for the ICA book *Excellence in Brand Communication*.

*Jonathan Knowles*

Jonathan's career has involved an equal amount of years on either side of the Finance and Marketing divide, leading *BusinessWeek* to call him "one of those rare financial guys who understands and appreciates marketing," and *MarketingNPV* to dub him "brand strategist extraordinaire with an unusual fluency in Finance." Jonathan just thinks of himself as being in the business of making companies more successful. His finance experience was gained with the Bank of England and with Marakon Associates, the value-based strategy consultants. His marketing derives from his time with Wolff Olins, the branding and corporate identity firm, and with BrandEconomics, the joint venture between Young & Rubicam and Stern Stewart. Jonathan now heads two brand consulting firms—Structured Intuition (based in Toronto) and Type 2 Consulting (based in New York). Jonathan was co-author of the ICA report "Measuring and Valuing Brand Equity," which included the first ever ranking of the most valuable brands in Canada. His articles on the role of brands in business have appeared in the *Harvard Business Review, Sloan Management Review* and *The Wall Street Journal*.

# PART 1

# FINDING COMMON GROUND

To put our topic in context, let's begin with this observation from David Aaker and Erich Joachimsthaler about the challenge of Marketing Accountability:

> *The brand leadership paradigm focuses on building assets that will result in long-term profitability, which is often difficult or impossible to demonstrate. Brand building may require consistent reinforcement over years, and only a small portion of the payoff may occur immediately—in fact, the building process may depress profits in the short run. Further, brand building is often done in the context of competitive and market clutter that creates measurement problems...*
>
> *The challenge of justifying investments to build brand assets is similar to justifying investments in any other intangible asset. Although the three most important assets in nearly every organization are people, information technology and brands, none of these appear on the Balance Sheet. Quantitative measures of their effect on the organization are virtually impossible to obtain; as a result, only crude estimates of value are available. The rationale for investment in any intangible asset, therefore, must rest in part on a conceptual model of the business that is often not easy to generate or defend. Without such a model, though, movement towards brand leadership is inhibited.*
>
> David Aaker and Erich Joachimsthaler, *Brand Leadership*

Nobody said it was going to be easy.

# Chapter 1.1
# Accountability and ROI

**What's in a name?**
*~William Shakespeare*

In the Marketing and Advertising worlds the term "ROI" has become a catch-all for Accountability. So the statement, "We need to know the ROI of our advertising" means, "We need good metrics on our advertising, short and long term, to show if we are making a sensible investment or not."

From a Finance point of view, though, the catch-all meaning is too broad. ROI is a *ratio* and it has a horizon of no more than 12–18 months:

$$\frac{\text{Funds Generated} - \text{Funds Invested}}{\text{Funds Invested}}$$

This makes ROI useful for comparing the return of one reasonably short-term investment to another, but it has to be used with care:

1. Given that it is a short-term concept, ROI is not suitable for assessing long-term brand-building effort.[1]

2. Given that it's a ratio, high ROI is not the same as optimal profit. You can get a numerically high ROI by investing very little. Tim Ambler shows that it is often better to consider absolute profit, i.e. Funds Generated minus Funds Invested. (See "ROI is dead; now bury it." *Admap 2000.*)

3. When Marketing and Advertising misuse "ROI" they reinforce a (wrong) Finance perception that their contribution is short-term and tactical. This is self-inflicted punishment, because it dilutes recognition that marketing and advertising effort builds brands as long-lived strategic assets.

---

1  Where the time exceeds 18 months, use of Net Present Value is more appropriate because it can accommodate a significant time lag between the investment and the return.

In terms of the impact on the business, marketing has a two-fold goal. First, to deliver short-term cash flow, usually in the 12-month planning period or the given fiscal year. Second, to create, sustain and grow the brand as an asset. Both are essential components of Accountability. With this in mind, we can diagram what to measure as follows:

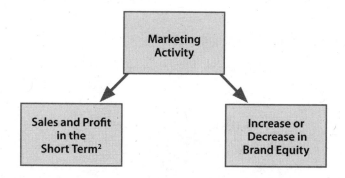

**Figure 1.1 – 1. The Two-Fold Measurement of Marketing Activity**

As noted, ROI is suitable for measuring the results in the left-hand box, but it's ill-suited to assessing Brand Equity. And given that major brands have values in the billions this separate treatment of Brand Equity is no small point.

It's also worth noting that the short- and long-term approach in the diagram parallels the way Finance people think about the Income Statement and Balance Sheet. This parallel is good, because it starts the process of finding common ground.

Finally, there's the question of language.

The wrong use of "ROI" really grates on some people. Just ask Tim Ambler.[3]

To prevent this, we recommend referring to "return" or "short and long term return" according to the circumstances.

---

2  In this book "short term" means "in the current fiscal year" or "in 12–18 months or so." "Long term" means "a year or more into the future," or "well out into the future."

3  We used the catch-all meaning in our title. Tim showed his displeasure by his pithy review comment: "Stupid title. Intelligent book!"

# Chapter 1.2
# A Trilingual Story

We are writing to three main audiences:

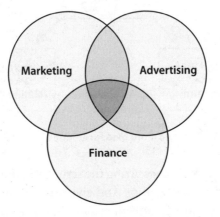

**Figure 1.2 – 1. The Three Main Audiences**

This means that certain topics will be new to some readers, but could look like déjà vu to others.

There'll be a temptation to skip the apparently familiar material, but we ask you to resist that. One of our objectives is to establish common language between the disciplines. So we ask you to read all the chapters. Most of them are a quick read, and we've added new perspectives throughout.

# Chapter 1.3
# No Simple Answer

> **At the heart of every complex problem is a simple answer—which is wrong.**[4]
> ~H.L. Mencken

We live in a world that obsesses on simplicity. Politicians reduce intricate policies to snappy sound bites. Presidential campaigns run on catchphrases. Business leaders struggle to articulate their version of what George Bush Snr. called the "vision thing."

All of this has its place, but it comes with dangerous baggage.

When issues are genuinely complex it can be hard to muster the drive, stamina and long-term commitment needed to solve them. For example, some readers will have felt a shiver of disagreement at Mencken's comment, wanting a simple way to deal with Accountability. But there isn't one.

Tim Ambler uses a vivid analogy. We wouldn't dream of expecting a single test, with a single magic number, to tell us that we are in good health. Equally, it takes several measures—and judgment—to determine the health of a brand or business.

Perhaps we should be glad it's tough.

In any field, the world's best don't ask for it to be easy. They *want* the bar high, because that's their chance to excel.

We can apply the same thinking to Accountability. It's not easy to get successful collaboration between Finance, Marketing and Advertising.

But think of the competitive advantage when you do achieve it.

---

4  We've used the popular version of quotations if the academically correct one is unfamiliar.

# Chapter 1.4
# What Business Are You In?

> **In this life, one thing counts.**
> **In the bank, large amounts.**
> *~Oliver—the Musical*

A company, appropriately enough, puts the priority on the bottom line. But, as Theodore Levitt stressed with his famous question, it must also have a clear idea of exactly what business it is in.

It would be instructive to compare the answers that Finance, Marketing and Advertising would give to this question. About the only thing we can say for sure is that they would not be unanimous. Partly, this is because the three disciplines have different responsibilities. But there is more to it than that. They often (in fact almost always) have a different world view of what the business is all about.

In some ways, differences are good. Cross-pollination and debate encourage innovation, while in-breeding weakens the bloodlines. But ultimately there must be a shared vision. We think it has to be:

### We Are in the Shareholder Value Business.[5]

Some Marketing and Advertising readers will bridle at this. They may quote Peter Drucker's maxim that the purpose of business is to create and keep customers. They would be right, in the sense that Customer Value is a prerequisite to Shareholder Value. But it is only a means to an end.

Others will point out that there is no simple "line of sight" between marketing or advertising activity and stock price. This is also true. However, Shareholder Value is the goal that Finance, Marketing, and Advertising can all share, because it shows that the resources of the business are being wisely invested.

---

5  We mean the Advertiser's Shareholder Value. Agencies have their own shareholders to satisfy, of course. But agency success depends on client success.

# Chapter 1.5
# Words, Words, Words

**What we've got here is failure to communicate.**
*~Cool Hand Luke—the Movie*

Even with agreement on Shareholder Value as the goal, we still have to deal with the fact that Marketing and Advertising people rarely if ever use Finance language.

They talk about Awareness, Insight, Preference, Loyalty, Cutting through the Clutter, Resonating with the Consumer, Every Point of Contact, Buzz, Viral Marketing, Total Customer Experience, etc. And when they talk about brands the floodgates open. There's Brand Essence, Brand Identity, Brand Image, Brand Personality, Brand Equity, Brand Value, Brand Truth, Brand Soul, Brand Health, and even Trustmarks and Lovemarks.

Finance live in the grittier world of Cash Flow, Market Capitalization, Earnings per Share, Return on Investment, Return on Assets, Value Creation and—as we will cover later—Profit, Growth and Risk.

This lack of a common language is a major cause of Vulcan-Earthling dissonance.

Fortunately, the two worlds do meet, because well-marketed brands, over time, improve all the financial indicators of the company.

# Chapter 1.6
# The Two Meanings of Value

| | |
|---|---|
| **Sprechen Sie Finanz?** | |
| | *~J. Kuppen* |

To Marketing and Advertising, value is seen through the eyes of the customer. It's the perceived overall benefit in relation to price.[6] To Finance, value is seen though the eyes of the company. The price received for delivering a product has to exceed, to a satisfactory degree, the cost of producing it.

These are two solitudes. Marketing and Advertising feel that Finance don't appreciate what it takes to win over the customer. Finance feel that Marketing and Advertising are out of touch with the economic consequences of their actions. In summary:

| Marketing/Advertising | Finance |
|---|---|
| *Equity* is something that a brand has. | *Equity* is something that a shareholder has. |
| The focus is on the overall benefit to the customer. | The focus is on business efficiency. |
| The goal is to create preference. | The goal is to generate profit. |

The "customer" and "company" views are both valid, but neither goes far enough. Focusing to excess on the customer could bankrupt the company. Focusing to excess on cost may improve short-term efficiency but will eventually lose the customer.

*Successful Accountability needs people to be fluent in each other's language; to understand what creates value for customers; and what delivers financial results for the business.*

[Note: In this book we are using "customer" or "consumer" according to the context. See the Glossary for a more detailed explanation.]

---

6 The word "value" needs to be used with care. A Jaguar is "good value" to those who think the benefits outweigh the price. But they won't describe their car this way because in everyday English "value" has a low-price and even low-quality connotation.

# Chapter 1.7
# Vulcans and Earthlings

> **That's not logical.**
> ~Mr. Spock

It's now time to dig deeper into our topic, and uncover why all the differences of opinion exist. It's because we do business on Earth, not Vulcan.

Vulcans are supremely intelligent and logical.

On Vulcan, the name of a product says what it does. Advertising lists facts. No one earns a handsome living hunting down Brand Truths and turning them into Big Ideas. Vulcans don't fall for the frippery that works with Earthlings. Logic is all.

As a result, there are no brands on Vulcan. Just functional products and services with functional names.

On Earth, it's utterly different. Earthlings are influenced by far more than pure facts. We are swayed by perceptions, and what other people think. We buy things for reasons (or feelings) that a Vulcan would find illogical.

There's probably an evolutionary explanation. When our ancestors, clad in skins and armed with spears, found themselves facing a sabre-toothed tiger, they needed more than logic to work out what to do. And it's worth noting that two of our most important life decisions (the person we marry and the house we buy) are heavily influenced by the emotional side of our nature.

This is crucial to our topic because of the different world views we talked about earlier in Chapter 1.4.

At their worst, the stereotypes are totally counterproductive. Finance see Marketing and Advertising as loose cannons, with a dangerous penchant for spending, and precious little idea about the realities of business. Marketing and Advertising sees Finance as bean-counting spoilsports with no imagination and no understanding of the customer.

There's a significant upside if Finance, Marketing and Advertising each acknowledge the value of each other's perspective.

To Finance, we ask you to redefine your frame of reference:

- Recognize that customers usually do not use pure logic and reason when they buy, and that they are often not ready, willing, or able to weigh every option according to its functional merits.
- Accept that customers value a mix of functional, financial, social and emotional benefits. (They are Earthlings, after all.)
- Allow for the fact that when Marketing and Advertising have ideas that you think are off the wall, they may just have discovered a source of breakout growth for the business.

To Marketing and Advertising, we ask you to appreciate that Finance has entirely reasonable requests. They want:

- A Causal Model, with identified assumptions, to explain how marketing and advertising effort contributes to business success, short and long term.
- A willingness on your part to put those assumptions to the test, and to adapt your plans in the light of the findings.
- Recognition that although the long term is important, so too is the short term.
- Agreed metrics for correlating marketing activity with financial outcomes.[7]

This is going to take effort. To put it bluntly, Finance are saying it's time for Marketing and Advertising to live by the Total Quality Management and Six Sigma approaches that drive virtually all other areas of business. Marketing and Advertising are saying that an overly numbers-driven approach—particularly if misused—will kill the innovation and creativity that is the lifeblood of the business.

However, all the evidence points to a sizeable upside for companies that get this dialogue right. So with that in mind, let's move to getting a shared understanding of brands.

---

7  This is the major focus of Part 3.

# Chapter 1.8
# Agreeing What Brands Are

> **A product is made in a factory.**
> **A brand is made in the mind.**[8]
> ~*Variously attributed*

Some people use *brand* and *product* interchangeably. But they are not the same. To highlight this, let's look at some history on Tide.[9]

A Vulcan would see Tide as a very good detergent—the best at getting clothes clean from a purely functional point of view.[10] Tide was also produced very cost-effectively, thanks to the ever-present effort of Procter & Gamble's Buying and Manufacturing departments.

This gave Tide a big advantage. But where does *product* stop and *brand* begin? Consider sudsing level. It's not related to cleaning, though most consumers think it is. So P&G spent time and money finding the sudsing level that *signalled* great cleaning. In a similar way, brighteners have no cleaning ability in themselves, though they make clothes *look* cleaner. How much should they be used, especially given their expense?

What about perfume? Originally, powders had floral perfumes. Then Lemon Sunlight hit on the fact that scent could signal cleaning ability. And even the texture of the granules mattered. Too fine, and they left an impression of weakness. Too coarse, and users worried that Tide wouldn't dissolve.

To some, these are product issues, but notice the words *signal, look* and *impression.* We are talking about perceptions here, not strict functional reality. They are brand issues.[11]

Going beyond these distinctions, there's also the question of what a brand stands for.

---

8 It has to be imprinted in long-term memory. This is a strength of effective advertising.
9 David R. was once the Tide Brand Manager.
10 Absolutes like "the best" are never strictly true—in that specialist products may beat the main brand in some narrow area. That said, Tide was better than all its main competitors.
11 Try this test. If it matters to an Earthling, but not a Vulcan, it's a brand issue.

Historically, Tide hammered away at cleaning, and only cleaning. Anyone who suggested it might stand for whitening, or brightening, or anything else, was quietly blindfolded, escorted off the P&G premises, and shot.[12]

Charles Revson of Revlon came at this another way. He said: *In the factory we make cosmetics, but in the store we sell hope.* This underlines the idea that a brand is a combination of reality and perception that is "more" than the product. This leads to the following definition, which we've created from existing ideas, and our own experience:

> *A brand is "more" than a product. It's a bundle of meanings—both rational and emotional—in the mind. To be successful, a brand must be seen as relevant, different and worth it by a big enough audience, who then buy it in preference to their other choices.*[13] [14]

As for getting the story out, this takes place at "every point of contact" with the audience. It involves the product in use, packaging, advertising, promotion, word of mouth, blogs, customer service, the impression created by the people that use the brand, the state of company trucks hurtling down the highway, and so on. The diagram shows this in a simplified way:

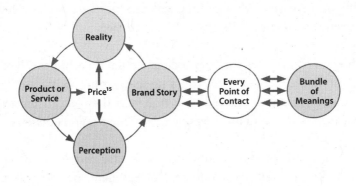

**Figure 1.8 – 1. A Brand is "More" Than the Product or Service**

Adapted from *Excellence in Brand Communication*

---

12 This fanatical belief in single-mindedness has since broadened. See Chapters 2.2 and 2.3.
13 Even though a brand is a bundle of meanings it will fail if it tries to be all things to all people. Keeping a brand "relevant, different and worth it" is a constant challenge.
14 "Other choices" include indirect ways of meeting a need, or not buying at all.
15 Price straddles reality and perception—especially in brands where high price signals prestige.

For decisions about the basic product or service, a Vulcan world view is good. Experience shows that it's downright dangerous to think that marketing and advertising can gloss over the shortcomings of a product—just ask North American automakers.

On the other hand, we must also think like Earthlings. On Vulcan, Coke is just a sweet fizzy brown liquid. On Earth, as we will learn in the next chapter, it has a brand value of between $US44 billion and $US65 billion.

# Chapter 1.9
# Agreeing That Brands Are Valuable

> **A billion here and a billion there, and pretty soon you're talking real money.**
> *~US Senator Everett Dirksen*

Here are the benefits of having a strong brand. Note that they address the priorities of both the Marketing and Finance departments:

a) Winning the battle for the consumer's mind.
b) Being bought in favour of competitors.
c) Enjoying higher customer loyalty.
d) Creating a barrier to entry, and blunting competitive attack.
e) Facilitating brand extensions.
f) Motivating staff and attracting new talent to the company.
g) Commanding a higher price.
h) Delivering current and future cash flow.
i) Delivering higher profitability.
j) Doing the previous two at lower financial risk.
k) Lowering the cost of borrowing.
l) Augmenting the stock price.

## Blind and Identified Tests

These give clear evidence of brand value. In the identified leg, the preference always shifts to the stronger brand, as in this example:

|  | Coke | Pepsi | No Preference |
|---|---|---|---|
| Preference (blind): | 44 | 51 | 6 |
| Preference (identified): | 65 | 23 | 12 |

**Table 1.9 – 1. Coke versus Pepsi (Blind and Identified Testing)**
Source: De Chernatoy and Knox, 1990

What causes the shift? The "moreness" embodied in the brand.[16]

---

16 Brad Davis of Wilfrid Laurier notes that in the identified leg the brain's reward centres lit up for Coke, i.e., respondents were "consuming" positive memories and associations.

In services the pattern is the same. Suppose you have to get an important package delivered. The AAA Delivery Guys may—to a Vulcan—be just as reliable as UPS, FedEx or Purolator, but an Earthling doesn't choose them, even though they are the first name in the *Yellow Pages*.

### Brand Valuation

"Moreness" can be calculated in financial terms. Interbrand has a list that appears in *BusinessWeek* each year. Millward Brown, using a slightly different methodology, has a rival ranking in the *Financial Times*. We reproduce their respective top 15 brands below:

| Rank | Interbrand | Brand Value ($US billions) | Millward Brown | Brand Value ($US billions) |
|---|---|---|---|---|
| 1 | Coca-Cola | 65.3 | Google | 66.4 |
| 2 | Microsoft | 58.7 | General Electric | 61.9 |
| 3 | IBM | 57.1 | Microsoft | 55.0 |
| 4 | General Electric | 51.6 | Coca-Cola | 44.1 |
| 5 | Nokia | 33.7 | China Mobile | 41.2 |
| 6 | Toyota | 32.1 | Marlboro | 39.2 |
| 7 | Intel | 31.0 | Wal-Mart | 36.9 |
| 8 | McDonald's | 29.4 | Citibank | 33.7 |
| 9 | Disney | 29.2 | IBM | 33.6 |
| 10 | Mercedes | 23.6 | Toyota | 33.4 |
| 11 | Citi | 23.4 | McDonald's | 33.1 |
| 12 | Hewlett–Packard | 22.2 | Nokia | 31.7 |
| 13 | BMW | 21.6 | Bank of America | 28.8 |
| 14 | Marlboro | 21.3 | BMW | 25.8 |
| 15 | American Express | 20.8 | Hewlett-Packard | 25.0 |

**Table 1.9 – 2. Brand Value Rankings by Interbrand and Millward Brown**

Source: Interbrand, *BusinessWeek:* July 2007. Millward Brown, *Financial Times:* April 2007

While the valuations on certain brands are different it's clear overall that brands are significant corporate assets. The Brand Value on these lists accounts for approximately 20% of the market value of the parent companies.[17][18]

---

17 Brand Value should not be confused with market capitalization (the share price times the number if shares outstanding). At the time of writing (November 2007) Coca-Cola has a market capitalization of US$140 billion and Google is valued at $220 billion.
18 For the latest Canadian rankings, see www.brandfinance.com/docs/news.asp

### Takeovers and Mergers

In the 1980s, Nestlé bought Rowntree for five times book value, and Philip Morris bought Kraft General Foods at a multiple of six. More recently, P&G valued Gillette at a multiple of ten. In other words, when strong brands change hands, they do so at several times their "Vulcan" value.

### Is It Worth Doing?

There's still the general question, however, of whether it pays to build a brand. The leaders of major brand companies certainly believe it does (see the John Pepper quote in Chapter 2.7), though they know that there is no "divine right of brands" guaranteeing success every time.

On the academic front, David Aaker and Robert Jacobson were among the first to attempt rigorous proof, and released confirmatory findings in 1994.[19] More recently, Madden, Fehle and Fournier published results that extend Aaker-Jacobson. For the six years through December 2000 they show that a portfolio of strongly branded companies outperformed the general market by over 40%, and at lower than average risk.[20]

**Figure 1.9 – 3. The Performance of Strongly Branded Companies**
Source: Madden, Fehle and Fournier (2006)

In Chapter 2.11 we review additional work by BrandEconomics and by Mizik and Jacobson that shows a strong correlation between brand health and financial performance.

With the general value of brands established, we turn to Brand Equity.

---

19 They found that movements in stock prices were affected both by changes in short-term returns and by changes in perceived quality.
20 For the statistically minded, the beta was 0.85.

# Chapter 1.10
# Brand Equity—Marketing and Advertising Version

> **It's not the man in your life that counts.**
> **It's the life in your man.**
>
> *~Mae West*

Companies have believed in brands for well over a 100 years.[21] However, the idea of Brand Equity did not arrive until twenty or so years ago. It gave "moreness" a financial aura, which was good—though it's worth noting that Finance people are not especially impressed when non-Finance people kidnap and manipulate their terminology.[22]

As a concept, Brand Equity is intuitively valuable, but hard to pin down. Tim Ambler calls it "what we carry around in our heads about a brand." David Aaker assesses it on the four dimensions below, and defines it as "the brand assets (or liabilities), linked to a brand's name and symbol, that add to (or subtract from) a product or service."

| Brand Awareness | Perceived Quality | Brand Associations | Brand Loyalty |

Aaker's boxes are essentially a de-constructed way of looking at "what we carry around in our heads," though Loyalty adds an element of behaviour.[23]

Virtually all marketing and advertising effort is trying to influence one or more of these areas, but Finance still needs to be convinced that the investment will deliver financially. This points up the need for a financially driven concept of Brand Equity.

---

21 Ivory Bar once had the decidedly Vulcan name of "White Soap." Harley Procter of P&G came up with "Ivory" in 1879, after hearing a biblical reference to "ivory palaces" in a sermon.
22 We urge against this borrowing, e.g., re-naming ROI as Return on Involvement, etc.
23 In Part 3 we make the point that it's behaviour that puts money in the bank. And speaking of banks, they illustrate that loyalty is complicated—in that a lot of customers are behaviourally loyal, while attitudinally grinding their teeth.

# Chapter 1.11
# Brand Equity—Finance Version

> **A brand is a long-term asset, fighting for its rights in a short-term world.**
> *~D. McWilliam*

Tim Ambler has a powerful metaphor to put Brand Equity in financial terms. He pictures it as a reservoir of cash flow, earned as a result of prior effort, but not yet released to the Income Statement.

**Figure 1.11 – 1. Ambler's Reservoir**

This bridges the worlds of Marketing, Advertising and Finance; referencing the goodwill accumulated through past actions, but highlighting that it will only become cash flow when it causes customers to spend money.

Ambler goes on to say that the reservoir can be drawn down to a greater or lesser degree to meet the demand for short-term profit. He cautions, though, that the reservoir has to be replenished, or the brand will suffer—and may even become "permanently dysfunctional."

The great value of this metaphor is that it puts the result of "what we carry around in our heads" in cash flow terms, and this is something that Finance people rarely if ever hear from their Marketing and Advertising colleagues.

Overall, it's a powerful way to start linking how Marketing, Advertising and Finance interact with each other, and we'll now build on this.

# Chapter 1.12
# The Idea of Utility—Removing Some Myths

> **Find the greed, and fill the need.**
> *~Jerry Goodis*

Peter Drucker articulates the concept of utility in this long quotation:

> *It is the customer who determines what a business is. It is the customer alone whose willingness to pay for a good or service converts economic resources into wealth, things into goods. What the business thinks it produces is not of first importance—especially not to the future of the business and to its success... What the customer thinks he is buying, what he considers value, is decisive. It determines what a business is, what it produces, and whether it will prosper. And what the customer buys and considers value is never a product. It is always utility, that is, what a product does for him.*[24]

Academic evidence and our Earthling-Vulcan analysis show that human beings want utility, and that utility consists of more than just functional benefits. Factors like status, trust, belonging and self-image also combine with product performance and price. It's a complex equation, but one thing is clear: utility leads to customer preference, and this drives premium margins and growth.

This should be common ground. But to make sure that Finance embrace utility, we have to debunk the myth that Emotion is somehow less valid than Reason as the basis for human behaviour.

The myth arises when people with a "logic and reason" view think, and sometimes say, that marketing and advertising effort is just a distraction for customers, covering up the inadequacies in a product.

---

24 Marketing and Advertising people will recognize *utility* as the functional, emotional and self-expressive benefits of a brand.

It shows again in the logic and reason belief that superior products will sell themselves, and don't need marketing support—despite all the evidence to the contrary.

When it comes to what influences people to buy, Reason and Emotion are different, but they are both powerful contributors to what customers see in brands. Reason asks, "does this product meet my needs on a functional level?" Emotion asks, "is this brand right for me?"

Today, it is becoming increasingly important to meet emotional needs because Total Quality Management and Six Sigma have narrowed the functional differences between products. The result is that customers are finding it harder and harder to identify the best product on function alone. The added values of a brand tip the scale.

That's not to say it's easy.

Reebok believed that their brand equity was strongly associated with exercise and wellbeing, rather than just sports shoes. So in 2001 it seemed natural to exploit this equity by launching Reebok Fitness Water. Consumers saw things differently, however, and failed to see the attraction of drinking water from a sneaker. The product has since been withdrawn.

On the other side of the coin, take a stroll around Home Depot and look at the most functional of categories—tools. They come in a huge array of shapes, sizes, and colours—all designed to enhance appeal through non-functional added values.

In summary, utility is rooted in the idea that consumers get value from tangible *and* intangible sources. This is directly parallel to what has happened in the valuation of companies, and this is where we turn now.

# Chapter 1.13
## The Idea of Intangible Assets

> **The other day upon the stair,**
> **I met a man who wasn't there.**
> **He wasn't there again today.**
> **I wish that man would go away.**
> ~*English Nursery Rhyme*

In general, as the nursery rhyme tells us, intangibles are not the easiest thing to grasp.

Finance people, on the other hand, are comfortable with the idea of intangible assets, because they define an asset as anything that is capable of producing cash flow now or in the future. It doesn't matter if it is a tract of land, a piece of machinery, a contract, a motivated workforce, an idea, or a brand. We'll explore this here, so that our three audiences can see things from a similar point of view.

### The Value of a Company
The value of a company comes from its tangible and intangible assets. The market puts a value on these, and reflects it in the stock price. This, times the number of shares outstanding, is the market capitalization. And this, plus the outstanding debt, is the Enterprise Value—what you would have to pay to buy the company i.e. all its assets, tangible and intangible.

### Tangible Assets
As the name suggests, tangible assets are "those that can be touched." They consist of land, buildings, machinery, raw materials, inventory and finished goods, and cash.

In 1978, according to *Fortune* Magazine, these assets accounted for 95% of the valuation of the companies in the Dow Jones Industrial Average. In line with this, our analysis for 1982 shows that the tangible assets of companies in the S&P 500 represented over 90% of their market value. By 2006, however, the "tangible" figure had declined to around 20%. What caused the change?

The answer, in a nutshell, is the emergence of the information economy in which intellectual property has replaced physical assets as the primary source of value creation. Baruch Lev, Professor of Finance and Accounting at the Stern School of Business, New York University, explains it this way:

> In the past few decades, there has been a dramatic shift in the production function of companies—the major assets that create value and growth. Intangibles are becoming substitutes for physical assets.

### Intangible Assets

Leif Edvinsson was a pioneer in the field of intangible assets and memorably defined them as "the ones that don't hurt when dropped on your toe." More formally, they are "those things that a company knows, has or does that make it worth more than just the sum of its tangible parts."

At any point, you can get a sense of the level of intangible assets in a company by comparing the market capitalization to its net asset value. The difference is intangible value. And over the last 20 years or so, intangible assets have taken on an increasingly important role.

The chart below plots the market capitalization of the companies in the S&P 500 as a multiple of their tangible assets. The current market-to-book multiple of 5 means that intangible assets now represent 80% of the value of these companies:

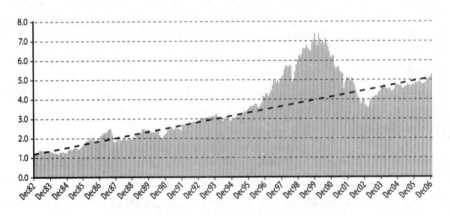

**Figure 1.13 – 1. The Growth of Intangible Assets**
Source: S&P 500 – Market-to-Book Ratio (Dec. 1982 – Dec. 2006)

This also shows when a company is taken over. There will be tangible assets like cash, property, plant and equipment, adding up to the net asset value. The purchase price, however, will be much more than this, as we noted earlier when we discussed Rowntree, Kraft General Foods and Gillette.

The difference is the Acquisition Premium. It is the value of the intangible assets, and has historically been designated as goodwill:

**Figure 1.13 – 2. Goodwill and the Acquisition Premium**

Edvinsson divided intangibles into structural and human capital, famously defining structural capital as "what remains when human capital goes home." This was problematic, though, because human capital does not legally belong to the company. So intangible assets are now defined as the intellectual property that is created by human capital, and that manifestly belongs to the company.

In 2004, the International Accounting Standards Board clarified the definition of intangible assets when it issued *International Financial Reporting Standard 3 (IFRS 3),* specifying how the goodwill arising in a merger should be accounted for. IFRS 3 requires companies to allocate the acquisition premium against the intangible assets being acquired.[25] It suggests five classes of intangible asset to consider:

- Marketing-related (such as trademarks and brands).
- Customer-based (such as customer lists).
- Artistic (such as movies and music).
- Contract-based (such as drilling rights and licensing agreements).
- Technology-based (such as patents).

---

25 Note that this only applies when there is a transaction. There is no provision for reporting the value of brands and other intellectual property that have been generated internally.

We can therefore look at the overall value of a company (its Enterprise Value) from a funding perspective (the value belonging to shareholders versus lenders) or an asset perspective (the tangible and intangible assets that it owns).

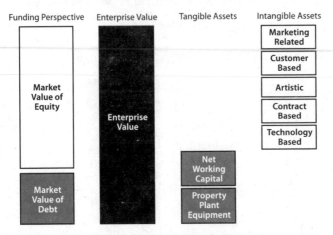

**Figure 1.13 – 3. The Value of a Company**

Note that intangible assets vary in importance by sector. In software and pharmaceuticals the main intangible value is in technology. For oil & gas companies, it's in contracts. For major advertisers, though, it is in the marketing and customer areas, and particularly in the value of their brands.

As we noted in Chapter 1.11, this value is defined by the reservoir of future cash flow that the Brand Equity represents, and that takes us to our next chapter, where we look at brands from a distinctly financial point of view.

# Chapter 1.14
# Profit, Growth and Risk

> **Once I built a railroad. Made it run.**
> **Made it run against time.**
> **Once I built a railroad. Now it's done.**
> **Buddy, can you spare a dime.**
>
> ~*Depression Era Song*

We've now reached a critical point in the book.

To Finance, value is all about cash flow; namely its level (Profit), its rate of change (Growth), and the certainty that it will be delivered (Risk).

This means that Profit, Growth, and Risk are dominant concepts in the Finance world. Yet Marketing and Advertising people rarely if ever talk in these terms.

This is a problem, but it's also a substantial opportunity. That's because strong brands have a significant impact on the three Finance priorities:

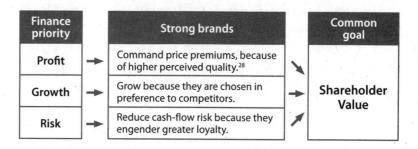

**Figure 1.14 – 1. Profit, Growth and Risk Related to Brands**

So, to Marketing and Advertising, we urge you to make Profit, Growth and Risk central to your mindset and vocabulary. To Finance, we urge you to encourage the effort that creates strong brands.

---

26 Some brands deliver profit through higher volume at a lower price.

# Key Points from Part 1

- Marketing, Advertising and Finance are all in the business of creating Shareholder Value.
- For effective collaboration, Marketing and Advertising need to talk in the language of Finance—and Finance needs to be conversant with the language of brands.
- Marketing and Advertising should be careful about using "ROI" as a catch-all term for Accountability. It can create the impression that their contribution is tactical, whereas brands are long-lived strategic assets.
- Accountability should be seen as a short- and long-term concept, dealing separately with short-term financial performance, and changes in Brand Equity.
- Brand Equity embraces the Marketing and Advertising notion of "what we carry around in our heads" and the Finance notion of "an asset capable of producing cash flows now and in the future." Tim Ambler's reservoir metaphor integrates the two perspectives.
- A successful brand is "more" than a product.
- The "moreness" occurs because brands appeal to Earthlings in ways that a Vulcan finds illogical.
- Successful brands have significant financial value because they deliver Profit and Growth at favourable Risk.

**Now we move to Part 2**

# PART 2

# WINNING HEARTS AND MINDS

In the Preface, we said that our objective is to get Finance, Marketing and Advertising onto the same planet, to the benefit of all concerned. We then devoted Part 1 to establishing common ground between the three disciplines—in particular, a shared interest in creating strong brands.

Here in Part 2 we change the focus, and ask Finance to step onto what may be unfamiliar terrain as we examine how Marketing and Advertising build strong brands.

There are no easy formulaic solutions, but there is one inescapable fact:

*Strong brands, using a combination of Vulcan and Earthling appeals, win the hearts and minds of customers better than their competitors do.*

# Chapter 2.1
# What Would Emerson Say?

> **Build a better mousetrap and the world will beat a path to your door.**
> ~Ralph Waldo Emerson

Emerson is describing a Vulcan view of the marketplace. But those days are long gone. True, innovations like iPod and BlackBerry still take the market by storm. But—as noted in Chapter 1.12—the majority of products are fighting to establish their merits on small functional differences. Reflecting this, here's what Emerson would have to say today:

> *Build a better mousetrap, but be aware that with today's media clutter you will have to work hard to make sure that your audience ever gets to hear about it. On top of that, be ready for the fact that competitors will quickly launch their own mousetraps, at least as good as yours. So, to stay competitive, a better mousetrap is essential, but it will not be enough. You have to go beyond product, and find ways to win the hearts and minds of customers. Do that, and the world will beat a path to your door.*

It isn't getting any easier, of course. Customers are increasingly savvy (some would even say cynical). And the internet can turn bad news into a tidal wave. Even so, the principles of success have not changed, and a famous example from the past will illustrate.

It's hard to imagine anything more functional than a muffler. But Speedy saw the power in an *emotional* appeal. They realized that when people went to the muffler shop they felt vulnerable. So they promised "At Speedy You're a Somebody." It doesn't focus on the functional side of mufflers at all. But it has been a great success.

This takes us to the Marketing Mindset—the next stop on our journey.

# Chapter 2.2
# The Marketing Mindset

> **The purpose of business is to create and keep a customer.**
>
> *~Peter Drucker*

Ever since Levitt wrote Marketing Myopia in the 60s, we've known that customers decide the fate of a company, voting with their feet. Customers may not always be right, but business (within reason) had better keep them happy.

This led to the idea of the Marketing Mix and the 4 Ps: Product, Price, Promotion, Place. (Product includes Packaging. Promotion includes Advertising. Place is synonymous with Distribution.)[1]

Later, the 4 Ps were augmented by the idea of Positioning.

For about thirty-five years, Positioning was built on the belief that a brand has to be single-minded. Volvo = Safe. Crest = No Cavities. Tide = Clean. This "one word" approach has since evolved (see later) but the Positioning decision is still crucial. It governs all the Ps, which today typically include the following:[2]

- Positioning
- Product
- Package
- Price
- Promotion [all forms]
- Place
- Pressure [$ spending, share of voice, etc.]
- People [resources, calibre, etc.]
- Process
- Profit

---

1  The Ps apply equally to Services, with adjustment to the meaning of Product and Package.
2  Brad Davis advocates 4 Cs—Customer focus, Cost, Communication, Convenience.

Marketing's job is to chart a winning path through all these Ps, taking competition and the market environment into account. It isn't easy, and there are cost-benefit trade-offs at every turn. Also Positioning, as a concept, has evolved.

Volvo is a cautionary example. Volvos *were* safe. They looked safe. They even sounded safe, with that reassuring *thwunk* when you closed the door. Advertising, promotion and product innovation all focused on safety. And with self-fulfilling symmetry, Volvo attracted people who were themselves safe. Solid, middle-class, sensible, and well-heeled.

This worked for years—so much so that Volvo became a poster child for the "one word" positioning philosophy.

Gradually, though, other carmakers upgraded their safety (real and perceived), and Volvo started to lose its distinctiveness. Worse, a dangerous downside emerged. Safety, for a stolid brand like Volvo, is a first cousin to dullness.

A problem like this won't be solved by a snappy ad campaign—and Volvo (a subsidiary of Ford since 1999) took the massive decision to re-tool. The goal: to make Volvos safe *and* exciting. Some see this is as an oxymoron that has to fail. Suffice to say that if it's successful, it will take years to know this for sure.[3]

Japan is another example of a huge long-term shift—this one successful. There was a time when "Made in Japan" meant a cheap shoddy knock-off. It took years of relentless effort, but we all know how the Japanese turned that perception around.

For Volvo and other brands the objective is still to win the hearts and minds of the right customers. But it's more complicated than it used to be.

The one-word idea of Positioning has given way to the multiple layers that make up a brand. To use a famous example, the "one-word" approach said Coke = Refreshment. It's clear that this falls a long way short of what Coke is all about.

---

3   At the time of writing Volvo is losing millions, and Ford is looking for a buyer.

This raises an associated point that we'll call "The Fallacy of the Clean Slate." When thinking about target audiences, it's wrong to assume that the consumer's mind is free and clear—uncluttered by pre-conceptions. The opposite is almost always true, and this has a profound effect on what needs to be done.

This book is not the place to go too deeply into this. However, to illustrate the point consider a brand that is well known and well understood, but still not doing well. There could be any number of reasons for this, but one is that consumers just aren't *interested* in what the brand has to say. If that's the case, hammering away at what people already know will not fix the problem. Consider Sunlight Laundry Detergent. People knew that it offered clean clothes at a sensible price, with a nice lemon scent. But this wasn't working. Something had to change, but what? Then they had a brilliant idea. For years, women had been harangued by advertising that told them to get clothes clean. But what's so terrible with getting dirty? They launched the "Go Ahead. Get Dirty" campaign, and the brand took off.[4]

A brand must still be "relevant, different and worth it," of course, and it must still be imprinted in long-term memory. But the focus has been shifting from the message that is *pushed at* consumers, to the more complex question of the impressions that they *retain*.

This has led to an evolution from the Marketing Mindset to the Brand Mindset.

---

4  For the full story, see the case library at www.cassies.ca. Sunlight won the Grand Prix in 1999.

# Chapter 2.3
# The Brand Mindset

> **The LORD set a mark upon Cain, lest any finding him should kill him.**
>
> ~*Genesis 4:15*

People in Finance can get a bit frosty over what they see as an overweening fuss about brands. We hope to melt some of that ice here, and as an opening comment we'll re-state the point made in Chapter 1.14—that strong brands are the common ground between Finance, Marketing and Advertising, *delivering Profit and Growth at favourable Risk.*

Branding has been around since the Garden of Eden. For those not familiar with the story, Cain was Adam and Eve's eldest son. In a fit of jealousy, he killed his brother Abel. It seems that God didn't believe in capital punishment, at least not then, perhaps because it would have ruined his population projections. In any event, he decided to banish Cain. You'd think Cain would go quietly, but he didn't. He complained that out there, wandering the face of the earth, he'd be on everybody's hit list. So, to protect him, God set a mark on him—making God the first Brand Manager.

Since then, branding has permeated our lives. It has been applied to products and services of course. It appears in self-improvement books like *The Brand Called You*. It is used all the time by political candidates. It has even been applied to countries, as when Tony Blair tried to re-brand Great Britain as "Cool Britannia."

Brands build up in our minds because of an Earthling compulsion—*to add meaning*. We do this even when that meaning is flimsy. We take a placebo, and it often has the same effect as a real drug. We see human characteristics in animals (anthropomorphism). We fall in love at first sight. None of these are rational, and they make a Vulcan shake his head.[5]

---

5  The placebo effect is so strong that a "placebo control" is mandatory in drug trials. A placebo would have no effect on a Vulcan, but with Earthlings the results can be astonishing.

Finance people will ordinarily not give this a lot of thought. Yes, Nike, Starbucks, Virgin, and Favourite-Example-Goes-Here are successful. But few are ready to attribute this success to anything other than sound operational management.

It does, however, go deeper.

In *A New Brand World* Scott Bedbury, former CMO of Nike and Starbucks, gives us a glimpse of the complexity of actually achieving this:

> *A brand is the sum of the good, the bad, the ugly, and the off-strategy. It is defined by your best product as well as your worst product. It is defined by award-winning advertising as well as the god-awful ads that somehow slipped through the cracks, got approved, and, not surprisingly, sank into oblivion. It is defined by the accomplishments of your best employee—the shining star in the company who can do no wrong—as well as by the mishaps of the worst hire you ever made. It is also defined by your receptionist and the music your customers are subjected to when placed on hold.*
>
> *For every grand and finely worded public statement by the CEO, the brand is also defined by the derisory consumer comments overheard in the hallway or in the chat room on the Internet. Brands are sponges for content, for images, for fleeting feelings. They become psychological concepts held in the minds of the public, where they stay forever. As such, you can't completely control a brand. At best you only guide and influence it.*

There's another factor too. Some years ago, leading thinkers noticed that people (in a parallel to anthropomorphism) see brands in human terms. One brand is a leader. Another a friend. Another trustworthy. And so on. This is Brand Personality, and it's important because consumers choose brands that they have a good *relationship* with.[6]

---

6 This has given rise to Customer Relationship Management—an approach that has had a chequered career (probably because there aren't many people who define a good relationship as being harangued by telemarketers at dinnertime).

This can all sound a bit wishy-washy to some. But imagine you are browsing in a store. A salesman invades your space—before you want him to—with a treacly, "Can I help you?" How do you feel? Your hackles go up.

This is an everyday example of how relationships affect sales. That's why Marketing, Advertising and Research people put so much blood, toil, tears and sweat into defining (a) what a brand is (b) what it can be (c) how to get it there (d) how to do so at reasonable cost. Here's a list of what has to be analyzed, understood and turned into something that works in the marketplace:

- Brand Essence
- Core Brand Identity
- Extended Brand Identity
- Brand as Product
- Brand as Organization
- Brand as Person

- Brand as Symbol
- Brand Value Proposition
- Brand Credibility
- Brand Relationship
- Brand Positioning
- Brand Building Programmes[7]

All of these contribute to the "bundle of meanings" referred to in Chapter 1.8. The challenge is to make it all come together. It's like the iceberg. The audience only sees what is above the water line, and the brand team has to simplify all the complexity.

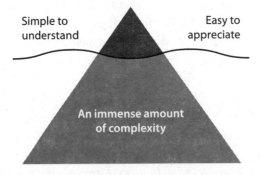

**Figure 2.3 – 1. The Iceberg Challenge for Brands**

---

7 The list is from Aaker's Brand Identity Planning Model. Bedbury (and most agencies) are more holistic in their approach. But all deal with similar concepts.

To do this, the starting point is to capture what the brand can and should stand for in a statement defining the *Brand Essence*. This, like all "brand" concepts, is excruciatingly hard to pin down. If you doubt it, get six people on the business to write their version, and see how far apart they are.

One reason is that a lot of "what we carry around in our heads about a brand" is non-verbal—feelings, impressions, visuals, snippets of music etc. Another comes from professional differences over what a Brand Essence statement should be like. Some want it short and pithy. Others want rich descriptions. Some believe that music and pictures are integral. Others say they are a distraction, and forbid anything but words.

These complexities can be worked through. The bigger challenge is how to capture what the brand stands for in a way that truly resonates with its audience. This has led to the following concept:

**Figure 2.3 – 2. Hitting the Sweet Spot**

Lisa Fortini-Campbell hit the sweet spot with her book of the same name. It urges marketers and agencies to find the core truth about their brand, and a unique way to express it. Though they weren't in marketing or advertising, Theodore Roosevelt and Marshal McLuhan had an instinct for this.

Roosevelt could have said, "We must move forward into the future with confidence," but he didn't. He said, "We have nothing to fear but fear itself."

McLuhan could have said, "Technology will make it easier and easier for everyday people, anywhere in the world, to interact with each other." Instead, he gave us the idea of the Global Village.

In a similar way, a brand must ring true in ways that have not been seen before. Nike is an inspirational example.[8]

The company started in the 1960s with Phil Knight and Bill Bowerman, who had a passion for serious athletics. They imported inexpensive top-quality running shoes from Japan, selling them at track meets, sometimes from the tailgate of Phil Knight's station wagon. Nike grew, but by the late 1980s had reached a tipping point. Sales were around $US800 million, but had recently declined, with Reebok taking over as #1 in the US.

Bedbury wrote in *A New Brand World*:

> *Every brand has at its core a substance that gives it strength. You have to understand it before you can grow it.*

Nike was positioned against the serious athlete. This was not a marketing ploy. It was a deep spiritual belief in the company. Some at Nike felt that broadening the appeal would kill the brand. Others felt that change was essential. Tough decisions had to be made.

Bedbury put these historic words in the Creative Brief for Wieden & Kennedy, Nike's advertising agency:

> *We need to grow this brand beyond its purist core. We have to stop talking just to ourselves. It's time to widen the access point. We need to capture a more complete spectrum of the rewards of sports and fitness.*

The fitness revolution was just starting, and Bedbury's words triggered a great insight at the agency: *that countless people, of all shapes and sizes, nurture athletic memories or dreams.* Like many insights, it may not seem so breathtaking after the fact, but it was brilliant nonetheless. And—essential for a sweet spot—it dovetailed perfectly with "the core substance, the fierce athletic heritage, that gave Nike its strength."

---

8  The Nike story will be past its sell-by date for some readers, but it is well worth retelling.

One thing remained. To find the right way say it. This, of course, became the legendary campaign expressing the idea:

*Just Do It.*

As Bedbury said, "The campaign transmitted a higher, more noble purpose. It was not about sneakers. It was about values. It was not about product. It was about a brand ethos."

This is the Brand Mindset. And a decade and a half later, Nike's sales are $US15 billion worldwide, and Reebok has fallen to such an extent that it has been taken over by Adidas.

At this point in the book we've covered a number of ideas. Perception and Reality. Bundle of Meanings. "Moreness." Vulcans and Earthlings. Logic and Emotion. Utility. Creating and Keeping Customers. Winning Hearts and Minds. Hitting the Sweet Spot. Making a Brand Relevant, Different and Worth It. Delivering Profit and Growth at Favourable Risk.

The Brand Mindset embraces all of these. It's about the entirety of how the company does business. It acknowledges the Vulcan requirement for quality in the functional product, the Earthling attraction to "moreness," and the Finance requirement for superior performance in the short term, not just the long term.

With that in mind, we now address the sometimes vexed question of the short- and long-term impact of the effort.

# Chapter 2.4
# Short- and Long-Term Roles

> **Rome wasn't built in a day.**
> **True, but I wasn't in charge on that job.**
> ~*Civil Engineer's joke (one of very few)*

Here, we'll review some broader concepts of marketing. Then we'll examine marketing and advertising effort according to its short- and long-term effect.

### Typical Marketing Activity

A good marketing plan has most though not always all of the following:

- A clear vision of what the brand can, and should, stand for.
- An understanding of the brand's sweet spot.
- A product (or service) that is competitive from the Vulcan point of view.
- A well-balanced Marketing Mix.
- A well-chosen price, with appropriate distribution.
- Consumer promotion with specific goals. (Trial, retrial, pantry loading, rewarding current users, short-term boost, etc.)
- Trade Promotion, to the degree needed or demanded.
- Loyalty programmes.
- Advertising, through mass or specialty channels.
- Direct and Relationship Marketing.
- Web-based effort.
- Sponsorship. Product Placement. PR.
- Events. Buzz. Viral Marketing. Word of Mouth.
- Overall integration.[9]

---

9  This is not always so simple. Huggies was about to re-run a successful promotion—with cash, cars and trips as prizes. A new client decided that the prizes "should be true to the Huggies brand." The Promotion House said that this was all very nice, but that baby-related prizes would not have enough pull. The promotion ran with them anyway. It was better integrated. But it failed.

## *Marketing Plan—Guiding Principles*

The plan will also follow certain principles such as:

- Deliver current-year targets, *and* put the brand in good shape for future years.
- Win the hearts and minds of the right customers. (Some combination of current, lapsed and new users—at various stages of awareness, commitment and loyalty.)
- Find the most productive way to grow:[10]

  a) Attract new/lapsed users while holding on to current ones.
  b) Increase share of requirements. For example, if someone buys the brand six times out of ten, increase this to seven.
  c) Increase the rate of consumption. For example, get more Cruncho eaten at each breakfast, or get it eaten more often.
  d) Stimulate new usage. For example, get Cruncho eaten as a late night snack.

- Remember that it is more expensive to attract a new customer than keep a current one, often substantially so. However, without new customers a brand will erode.
- Recognize that brands have different levels of responsiveness e.g. the Stars, Dogs and Cash Cows of the Boston Consulting Group Matrix. However, remember that a (so far) unresponsive brand may, with new thinking, be a success waiting to happen.[11]
- Finally, though not a guiding principle, note that plans tend to be dominated by short- rather than long-term forces because of the Immediacy Effect—which we will discuss next.

---

10 This may involve line extensions, provided that cannibalization is taken into account. It also applies to services e.g. more people going to a restaurant, going more often, and spending more while there.
11 There is evidence in PIMS that brands, previously categorized as having low potential, can in fact do very well.

## *The Immediacy Effect*

This is a cousin of the Recency Effect: the tendency to treat the most recent information as the most important. With the Immediacy Effect, we give priority to *immediate* effects. For example, we offer price discounts because they clearly boost short term sales, even though we have strong evidence that price discounts can damage Brand Equity.[12]

We're writing this in the aftermath of the "Employee Pricing" war in the auto market. GM found a clever way to position a price cut, and sales responded. But Ford and Chrysler quickly copied, neutralizing the advantage. This leaves the longer-term effect on sales, profits and Brand Equity—especially when prices go back up—very much in question. Meanwhile, Toyota (a stronger brand) reported that sales continued to go up, with much less discounting.

A Vulcan would point out that the Immediacy Effect creates double jeopardy. It makes the short-term more attractive than it should be, *and* it diverts attention from long-term consequences.

With a promotion, for example, it comes as no surprise that the business goes up in the promoted period. But what about afterwards? Some of the lift comes from sales that the brand was going to get in the future, and at full price. This is why there is often a post-promotion loss in sales. To take this into account, it's essential to measure the *overall* effect of the effort.

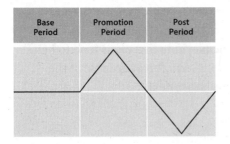

We say this because the post-promotion calculation does not seem to be especially widespread today. The immediate gain wins friends and influences people. But the subsequent trough doesn't seem to get the same level of attention.

**Figure 2.4 – 1. Promotion Trough Effect**

---

12 See Jadidi, K., et al. and Pauwels, K., et al. in the References.

### *The Measurability Effect*

David Ogilvy pointed out that if you lose your keys at night, you don't look for them under a lamppost just because that's where the light is. Yet a version of this is affecting marketing plans. Certain easy-to-measure tactics (e.g. Direct Response and Interactive) are getting increased investment. Meanwhile traditional advertising is under a good deal of pressure.

This shift is understandable, but it needs more thought. For example, there is ample evidence that advertising (along with good product) drives Brand Equity. Srivastava, Shervani and Fahey wrote a highly regarded paper on the topic. They put it like this:

> *Brand and Channel Equity reflect bonds between the firm and its channels and customers. The former [Brand Equity] is the result of extensive advertising and superior product functionality. The latter [Channel Equity] may be the result of long-standing and successful business relationships between the firm and key channel members.*[13]

In other words, the guiding principle needs to be "that which is best for the business" and not "that which is most easily measured."

### *"Short Term" Effect versus "Brand Building"*

In general, sales promotion, price and distribution affect short-term sales more so than advertising. In fact, it's quite rare for an ongoing brand to get an immediate and spectacular response to advertising. David Ogilvy claimed it for only a handful of his campaigns. Peter Elwood, former President of Lever and Lipton in Canada, says much the same.

This may explain a bad habit in our business—juxtaposing "short term" and "brand building" as opposites. An exchange between two colleagues in Direct Marketing and Advertising might go:

> "Are you expecting any short-term share lift from this effort?"
> "Not especially. It's a brand-building campaign."

---

13 Channel Equity can be extremely valuable, though on occasion a mixed blessing. Consider the relationship that Wal-Mart has developed or demanded with its key suppliers.

The reply is understandable given the Immediacy and Measurability Effects. But it's not right. It seems to say that brand building is some latent and esoteric force, invisible now, only waiting to reveal its effect in the future.

In reality, advertising *does* have a short-term effect, though it can be masked by the other factors. The effect is clear from Marketing Mix Modelling, which we'll come to later. It's also clear from the work of John Philip Jones. Using split cable tests, he finds what he calls Short-Term Advertising Strength (STAS). He shows that people recently exposed to advertising are more likely to buy the advertised brand than those not exposed.

This does not occur all the time, of course. A poor response may be due to weak creative. Or there can be an arm-wrestler standoff, where competing brands having strong but similarly effective creative. Or there may be price/promotion/distribution pressure. Also, as with many things to do with ad measurement, there are people who question Jones's conclusions (Leonard Lodish being one). But Colin McDonald reports that the results have been replicated with a similar methodology in the UK and Germany. So it seems that there's validity to the findings.[14]

It has to be said, also, that the short-term business response to advertising may not be enough to generate an immediate pay out. Even so, world adspend is $US650 billion a year, and it's unlikely that this comes from a compulsive desire to lose money. There must be more to the story. And this takes us back to the Two-Fold Measurement diagram on page 3:

**Figure 2.4 – 2. (A repeat of Figure 1.1 - 1)**

---

14 Jones also argues that one exposure is often enough to get a STAS response. This challenges "Effective Frequency" and has stirred up the media community, pro and con.

Advertising, done well, delivers in the short *and* the long term. It influences "what we carry around in our heads," thereby raising or replenishing the Brand Equity in Tim Ambler's reservoir. And *this* translates to Profit and Growth at favourable Risk.[15]

There remains one last point on "Short Term versus Brand Building," and it has to do with *when* successful advertising gets into our heads. This can be contentious because of what is called the wear-in effect.

There's universal agreement that successful advertising gets into our long-term memory in a brand-linked way. Some argue that this *can*, on occasion, happen via a slow build. The first Molson "I AM" campaign is an example. Apparently, it did not have much effect at first, because the target audience did not get the idea. Over time, though, they did, and the business eventually did extremely well—winning a Cassies Gold for effectiveness in 1997. Notwithstanding this, the more prevalent view is that a campaign has to establish itself early, or it will probably not establish itself at all.

This brings us full circle to the title of this section. Brand-building advertising *does* have a short-term effect, though it may be masked. And it definitely has a long-term effect. Given this, we recommend a slight but important change in semantics. We should stop using "versus" and think in terms of "Short Term *and* Brand Building Effect."

### Short- and Long-Term Roles

Anyone building a marketing plan wrestles with the balance between the short and long term. Although there are always exceptions, tactics can generally be categorized according to their short- or long-term effect, and we thought it would be useful to summarize that here. The first item may catch readers by surprise, because it often gets taken for granted.

---

15 We discuss overall profitability starting at Chapter 2.6—*Advertising as Investment*.

| Activity | Comment |
|---|---|
| Brand Equity, inherited as a result of previous effort; and reinforced or enhanced by current effort | Often the biggest single factor in delivering short- and long-term results (see Chapter 2.9) and the reason why we lay so much stress on Brand Equity in this book. |
| Positioning | Guides all immediate and long-term effort, and must be carefully chosen, managed and nurtured. |
| Product and Price (and to a lesser extent Packaging) | Affects the immediate and the long term i.e. if these core elements are out of kilter, the brand will suffer. |
| Distribution | The level affects the short and long term. Changes affect the short term. The type of outlet that carries the brand can also affect image in some categories e.g. salons vs. supermarkets for hair and beauty products. |
| Consumer/Trade Promotion | Mainly affects the short term, and if it has the feel of "giving the product away" may have a negative effect on Brand Equity. (Sampling will have a long-term effect if it helps a brand establish itself.) |
| Advertising | As noted in this chapter, it has a short- and long-term effect (though the short-term effect can be masked by other effort). |
| Direct Marketing (all versions, including Web-based effort) | Has an immediately measurable effect. It may also have long-term value (e.g. expanding the customer base) but it puts a priority on sales response over Brand Equity. |
| CRM/Loyalty | Usually designed with the short and long term in mind. |
| Sponsorship. Product Placement | Usually has short- and long-term objectives, based on image by association. |
| PR | Announcement PR tends to be short-term. Reputation PR tends to be long-term, though they obviously overlap. |
| Events. Buzz. Viral Marketing | Tend to be used short-term, but can have long-term carryover. |

**Table 2.4 – 1. Short- and Long-Term Roles**

With these as the main activities, the next topic is building a plan with the right balance.

# Chapter 2.5
# Choosing amongst the Possibilities

> **If I'd known I was going to live this long,
> I would have taken better care of myself.**
> ~Mickey Mantle

Mickey Mantle was haunted by the belief that he, like his father, would die young. He lived hard and drank hard, with no thought for the future. This led to alcoholism, cirrhosis of the liver, and liver cancer. Amazingly, though, he still lived into his 60s.

In contrast, brands must look ahead. They can survive a certain amount of abuse, but they need sustained and balanced support, with the short *and* long term in mind.

In an ideal world, we would be able to model this. We would know (a) what it takes to create and keep a customer (b) profitably (c) now and long term (d) in the face of competitive pressure, and (e) under various market conditions.

Furthermore, we would know what results to expect from different marketing tools—on their own, and in combination.

In fact, we are a long way from this, and it's worth listing why:

- There are just too many variables to measure.
- Good actionable information is hard and expensive to get.
- It takes time to build a model, and the market can change.
- Models are black boxes. This can raise doubts about their validity.
- People protect their turf, often making it difficult to get objective measurement of results.

Rust, Ambler, Carpenter, Kumar and Srivastava examined the challenge in their paper "Measuring Marketing Productivity." They say:

> *Chain-of-effects models, capable of addressing the strategic trade-offs across competing marketing expenditures, are much rarer.*

In non-academic language, this is saying that there is no science for allocating the budget across the marketing mix. So what *do* we have? There's Marketing Mix Modelling, though this has limitations, as discussed in Chapter 2.9. There are Media Mix models at some agencies and media companies. And there are single-source initiatives like Apollo. (This is a major attempt to relate purchases to media exposure. It's backed by some of the top names in packaged goods. See the Glossary.)

Larry Percy, in *Strategies for Implementing Integrated Marketing Communications*, tackles the question a different way. He assumes a sequential buying process and asks questions like: Are consumers aware? Aware but unconvinced? In the franchise, but not yet loyal? The answers suggest different tactics—though the amount to spend on each is still a judgment call. Alan Middleton, Laurie Young and Guy Stevenson outline a similar approach in *Excellence in Brand Communication*.

More broadly, packaged goods companies have been increasing trade spending—though driven more by trade demands than conviction that it is right for the brand. Direct Response and the Internet have also been increasing their share of the budget, along with increasing interest in sponsorship, product placement, buzz and guerrilla marketing.

Overall, though, there is limited guidance on budget allocation. Decisions are being helped by well-designed Marketing Dashboards and Brand Scorecards (see Part 3), but they often still rely on a good dose of history, experience and judgment.

### How Budget Allocations Would Ideally Be Made

In personal finance, we have yardsticks. (X% in fixed income, Y% in domestic equities, Z% in international equities etc.) Marketing is too complex for this, but we do have a *conceptual* answer—that the right allocation is the one that delivers the best balance between the short and long term.

It may help to assess proposed effort against the Accountability Matrix. It would be easy, of course, if all tactics fell in the NE quadrant—with a positive effect on short-term results *and* Brand Equity—but this is almost never the case. Some tactics deliver in the short-term, perhaps with a negative effect on Brand Equity. Others are better for Brand Equity, but the investment can depress short-term results.

Trade-offs will be needed, and the idea is to keep the activity in balance.[16]

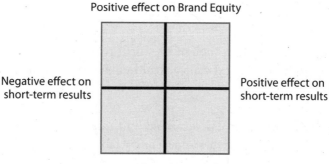

**Figure 2.5 – 1. The Accountability Matrix**

The right allocation still takes judgment. So we'll stress the point made earlier: that the answer is "that which is best for the business," not "that which is most easily measured."

---

16 A difficult question is the trade-off between brand building and price/promotion. Clearnet/ Telus took the long view, investing in building the brand, and avoiding competition on price. (See the Clearnet/Telus cases at www.cassies.ca—Gold winners for Sustained Success.)

# Chapter 2.6
# Advertising as Investment

> **I know half of my advertising is wasted.**
> **I just wish I knew which half.**
> *~See attribution below* [17]

You can hardly pick up a book on advertising without finding some version of this notorious quotation.

The connotation is negative, though it's worth remembering that Lever and Wanamaker both became extremely wealthy men, despite their apparently wasteful ways.

This bears thinking about. For example, imagine a Direct Response programme with a 3% response rate and a comfortably positive ROI.

No one says, "I know 97% of my programme is wasted. I just wish I knew which 97%." We know that the productive 3% covers the overall investment and more besides.

The same holds true for any venture that combines risk and reward. An oil company sinks many holes before it hits black gold. It doesn't condemn drilling because some of the holes come up dry.

In this sense, advertising has allowed itself to be blind-sided by a catchy quote.

It goes without saying that advertising has to do all that it can to drill in the right place. But the question is not whether some of the effort is wasted. It's whether the investment, as a whole, pays off.

The next four chapters examine this issue, but first we must lay some groundwork.[18]

---

17 Most probably said by William Hesketh Lever, the Lever in Unilever, but also frequently
   attributed to John Wanamaker, the US department store magnate.
18 In these chapters, advertising means effort that runs in TV, radio, print, outdoor, etc.

## No Universal Formula

There will be those who want a simple answer from the good old days of "It pays to advertise." After all, Einstein gave us $E = mc^2$ to describe the universe. How come no one can find a simple formula for the value of advertising—or marketing come to that?

It's not for want of trying. We referred earlier to the paper "Measuring Marketing Productivity." The distinguished authors have spent years looking into the question. Their paper acknowledges the complexity:

> There are three challenges to the measurement of marketing productivity. First, relating marketing activities to long-term effects. Second, separating individual marketing activities from other actions. Third, [accepting] that purely financial methods have proved inadequate for justifying marketing investments—non-financial metrics are also needed.

All of this stands in the way of an $E = mc^2$ type of answer. However, there's compelling evidence for what we might call the General Theory of Advertising Effectiveness, and that is what we will cover. The first step is to establish a framework for discussion.

## An Agreed Mental Model

We all have a sense of how advertising works, but whether we realize it or not our mental models can be very different.[19] This is what we are using:

- Advertising, by one means or another, gets into our heads.[20]
- It then affects what we think, feel and do—to varying degrees.
- The effect on "think and feel" is crucial, but it is a means to an end. To deliver cash flow, advertising must ultimately influence *what we do.*
- Some advertising works in the moment (e.g. a table-top ad in a restaurant for a new dessert). Most has to bridge a gap between when it runs and later purchase.

---

19 Paul Feldwick in the UK first said this. He also added a provocative thought. Given that there is no all-embracing answer, our own mental model can't be right all the time.

20 There are differences of opinion as to how this happens. Colin McDonald gives an excellent review in *Is Your Advertising Working?*

- It does this by getting into long-term memory, and it has to do this in a brand-linked way.[21]
- For advertising to have a long-term effect it must first have a short-term effect.[22]
- Successful advertising delivers short-term business results *and* it builds Brand Equity. This in turn delivers long-term results.[23]
- Spending matters up to a point, but creative (message + execution) has far more leverage than the brute force of media weight.
- The combined short- and long-term effect of advertising must be positive for Profit, Growth and Risk, i.e., when properly accounted for it must pay out.[24]

---

21 Promotional advertising is less concerned with long-tem memory. The same holds for Direct Response. It puts a higher priority on response than on the image left in the mind.
22 This is a majority view, but some argue that a spectacular long-term effect can come after a slow start.
23 Short-term results may be masked by price, promotion, competition, etc. See Chapter 2.4.
24 This assumes appropriate effort to measure long-term effects.

# Chapter 2.7
# Advertising's Impact on Profitability

> **Give me a lever long enough, and I will move the world.**
>
> ~Archimedes

*Synopsis: A major study in the late 90s shows a clear correlation between advertising effort and return. The study was based on 200+ companies—principally in branded consumer products—in the UK and Europe. It was commissioned by the IPA through PIMS.*[25]

First, it's worth recapping the "experience" argument for advertising and profitability. P&G has more #1 brands than any packaged goods firm in history, and John Pepper, then the President, said this in a 1988 speech:

> *I believe in advertising because I have seen throughout 25 years that the correlation between profitable—let me emphasize profitable—business growth on our brands and great advertising isn't 25 percent, it's not 50 percent, it's not 75 percent. It is 100 percent. And I don't deal in hyperbole here. In 25 years I haven't seen a single P&G brand sustain profitable volume growth for more than a couple of years without having great advertising. Great advertising alone won't do the job. We know that. The product must be right. The pricing must be right. We've got to provide superior satisfaction, superior value to consumers. But great advertising; it's purely and simply a must.*

P&G is a major world advertiser. However, a sceptic could still say, "That's fine for them, but does it apply to us?" The IPA study set out to answer such a question.[26]

The starting point was Perceived Quality, i.e., actual quality enhanced by the "moreness" that derives from marketing and advertising.

---

25 The IPA is the UK's advertising industry body—highly respected for its work. PIMS has been described by Tom Peters as "the most extensive strategic database in the world."
26 What follows draws heavily on Chapter 1 of AdValue, with our thanks to Leslie Butterfield.

David Aaker stressed its importance in *Building Successful Brands:*

> *Perceived quality is the single most important contributor to a company's ROI, having more impact than market share, R&D or marketing expenditures... (it) is usually at the heart of what customers are buying, and in that sense, it is a bottom-line measure of the impact of a brand...*

Through extensive analysis, the study found a clear and causal chain of effects relating advertising to perceived quality and ultimately to return:

*Advertising → Perceived Quality → Relative Customer Value → Return*

The first step can be seen in the chart below. It shows the correlation between Ad Spend and Perceived Quality (each relative to competition):

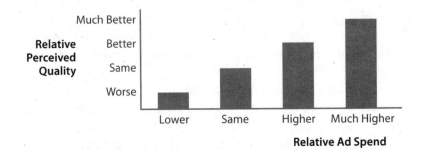

**Figure 2.7 – 1. Relative Ad Spend vs. Relative Perceived Quality**
Source: PIMS Europe Database—1998

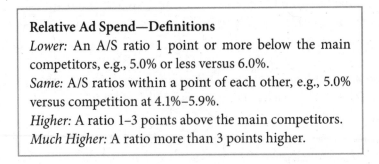

**Relative Ad Spend—Definitions**
*Lower:* An A/S ratio 1 point or more below the main competitors, e.g., 5.0% or less versus 6.0%.
*Same:* A/S ratios within a point of each other, e.g., 5.0% versus competition at 4.1%–5.9%.
*Higher:* A ratio 1–3 points above the main competitors.
*Much Higher:* A ratio more than 3 points higher.

As confirmation of the first step, the study also examined Product Image and Company Reputation (which are known to influence Perceived Quality). Again, there was a strong correlation with Relative Ad Spend:

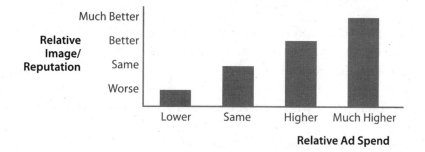

**Figure 2.7 – 2. Relative Ad Spend vs. Relative Image/Reputation**
Source: PIMS Europe Database—1998

Now, Perceived Quality, Image and Reputation—in relation to Price—drive Relative Customer Value. So the final step was to examine Relative Customer Value against ROI:

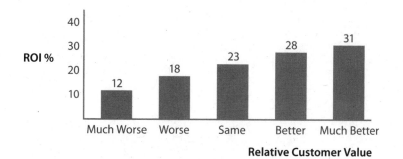

**Figure 2.7 – 3. Relative Customer Value and ROI**
Source: PIMS Europe Database—1998

This is powerful evidence of advertising's effect on financial returns.

There's one final question—causality. It could be argued that the companies in the first two charts *started* with better Perceived Quality, Image and Reputation—and chose to spend more as a result. Given how spending decisions get made, however, this hardly seems probable.

The more likely conclusion is that advertising (not always, but often) enhances Perceived Quality, which in turn enhances Relative Customer Value, which in turn enhances the financial return.

This is entirely in line with the academic findings discussed in Chapter 2.11.

Or, to put it in terms that Messrs. Lever and Wanamaker might appreciate, the "the half that works" is, in general, profitable enough to make the overall effort pay out.

# Chapter 2.8
# Advertising's Long-Term Effect

> **Gravity operates at a distance. But does anyone question that it works?**
>
> ~*The Astronomy Café*

*Synopsis: We know that advertising has a long-term effect, in that we all carry brand impressions that have been in our heads for years. It has been difficult to prove, however, that these impressions affect long-term sales. A massive study in the early 90s found the proof. It was based on test markets where the advertising effort occurred only in Year One. Even so, sales went up for three years, and the accumulated incremental volume was double the one-year figure.*

Some CEOs and CFOs (not unreasonably) want "test vs. control" evidence for the long-term value of advertising. It doesn't help when Marketing and Advertising people say, as they often do, that the latest attempt has turned out to be unreadable—polluted by factors beyond their control.

The fact is, however, that it is virtually impossible to run a valid test for one year, let alone three. That's why it has been so hard to get good long-term data—until the BehaviorScan study.

BehaviorScan run split-cable US test markets for top packaged goods clients. They had 400 tests in their databank. Clients had their own results, of course, but were aching to know what could be learned by pooling the information. Leonard Lodish and Beth Lubetkin published the results in 1992.

It's important to stress the rigour of this study. BehaviorScan had statistically matched households in ten US cities. In true scientific method, test and control households got the same marketing plan, except for the one difference being examined. This might be media weight, or creative, but not both. Media weight was basically all in television. Brands were also categorized as either established or new.[27]

---

[27] Households had meters and scanners to track media exposure and product purchase.

Remarkably, BehaviorScan found that they had 44 markets where a "test vs. control" comparison was available and valid over a three-year period.

These 44 markets all had a media heavy-up in Year 1, and this had led to an average 22% increase in brand volume versus control. In Years 2 and 3, however, the test and control areas got *exactly the same plan*. In other words, the only difference between the test and control markets occurred in Year 1, but the volume effect was readable over three years. In describing the results, the authors say:

> It has long been hypothesized that advertising can have a very significant long-term impact on sales. However, that has not in the past been supported by real empirical data. Today, we have the data that lays this issue to rest.

| Time | Effort vs. Control | Volume vs. Control |
|------|--------------------|--------------------|
| Year 1 | Heavy Up | + 22% |
| Year 2 | No difference | + 14% |
| Year 3 | No difference | + 7% |

**Table 2.8 – 1. Test vs. Control Volume Growth**
Source: Lodish and Lubetkin (1992)

The authors point out that the three-year effect (22% + 14% + 7%) is virtually double the one-year effect, and suggest that this should be taken into account when assessing payout.

It's not as catchy as their original quote but—faced with these results—Lever and Wanamaker could have said, "The cumulative three-year impact of my advertising is double the one-year effect."

# Chapter 2.9
## The Long Term, from Another Perspective

> **There are a million ways to skin a cat.**
> **Yes, but why would you need more than one?**
> ~Taxidermist Joke

*Synopsis: Hess and Ambach use Frequent Shopper Databases to uncover a long-term advertising effect that is, on average, somewhat more than double the level typically reported by Marketing Mix Modelling. Although the methodology is very different from BehaviorScan, the overall finding as to long-term effect is very similar.*

The Hess and Ambach premise is that Marketing Mix Modelling does not pick up long-term effects—and therefore does not give a complete picture for the effect of advertising.[28]

The argument unfolds as follows.

For years, it was difficult to relate marketing activity to in-store sales. Then scanners arrived, giving precise information. And at the same time, pricing, consumer/trade promotion, in-store display, distribution, advertising etc. were getting easier to track.

This made Marketing Mix Modelling possible. It uses sophisticated mathematics to isolate the cause and effect of change, and thereby extract the individual effects of different tactics. With proper data, a good model can produce a theoretical sales curve that closely fits the real one. It is also able to say that X% of incremental sales have come from advertising, Y% from price promotion, Z% from coupons, etc. Some models even look at what-if scenarios and evaluate the potential effectiveness of future marketing mixes.

This sounds like the Holy Grail. But there's a but.

---

28 For a paper on Marketing Mix Modelling and Econometrics, see Useful Links. For the Hess and Ambach paper, see the References.

Even though the model needs a long history of data (generally monthly for at least three years), it only deals with *short-term change*.

To use a finance analogy, suppose a million dollar portfolio increases by 5%. The model looks at what is causing change, but is "blind" to what is staying stable. This is a limitation of the mathematics, and it leads to results like those in this pie chart from the Hess and Ambach report:

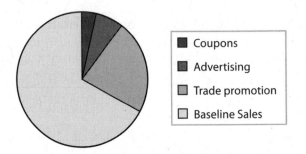

**Figure 2.9 – 1. Marketing Mix Model Results Reported by Hess and Ambach**

The top right hand quadrant shows the percent of the business—in terms of short-term cause and effect—that can be attributed to promotion, advertising etc. Note, however, that roughly two thirds of sales are not accounted for. To deal with this, Marketing Mix Modelling introduces the idea of "baseline sales." These are sales that, according to the mathematics, the brand was going to get anyway. Or, put another way, they are the sales that the brand would get in the given year if it closed down marketing investment.

But these sales don't materialize out of thin air. There has to be a driving force that the model is not picking up. It's the accumulated effect of past activities on the brand—experience with the product, advertising, promotion, pricing and so forth. In other words, the accumulated Brand Equity.

Hess and Ambach come to the reasonable conclusion that if Marketing Mix Modelling is not explaining roughly two thirds of what is going on, it must be missing something.

They rather wickedly point out that scanners (the basis for most Marketing Mix Models) are not very smart. A scanner can't tell if a customer is good or bad.[29] It can't tell if the sale is from a new, lapsed or loyal user. It doesn't know if users are buying more often, or more each time. And it can't tell if a customer is becoming more or less loyal.

Fortunately, they have a rich new data source—Frequent Shopper Databases— which do what scanners can't do. FSDs look at individual people. And Hess and Ambach had seven million US households to work with, as they delved into what Marketing Mix Models miss.

They found that advertising can have an effect in four ways, three of them long term:

1. *Short Term.* This is picked up by Marketing Mix Models.
2. *Purchase Cycle.* People who buy as a result of advertising use a brand up slightly faster than those who buy for other reasons.
3. *Repeat Rate.* Ad-induced buyers are more likely to become repeat buyers.[30]
4. *Buying Rate.* Ad-induced buyers tend to buy more often.[31]

They show this using a bar graph—and the following chart for a particular brand is extracted from their report.

**Figure 2.9 – 2. Short- and Long-Term Advertising Effect (Hess and Ambach)**

---

29 Not all customers are good. In any given category there are Promiscuous Price Shoppers who snap up brands at loss-leader prices, and have negative lifetime value for those brands.
30 For the brand in the pie-chart, there is a 50% repeat rate, versus 35% for purchases induced by trade promotion.
31 For the pie-chart brand it was 3.2 purchases/year, versus 2.6 for those induced by a trade deal.

The Short-Term Effect is the one picked up by Marketing Mix Models. The others are picked up by the Frequent Shopper data—and in this particular case the overall effect is 2.74 times the Marketing Mix Modelling Effect (19.20 ÷ 7.00 = 2.74). Hess and Ambach have repeated the study a number of times, and they summarize their findings as follows:

> *The multiplier for advertising's overall effect ranges from 1.58 to 3.98 of the Marketing Mix Model Effect, with an average multiplier of 2.32.*

This, and the BehaviorScan data, give clear evidence of advertising's long-term effect. And we can add that Millward Brown, the largest advertising tracking study company in the world, have come to a similar conclusion from their immense databases.[32]

---

32 Information provided by Bill Ratcliffe, former President of Millward Brown in Canada.

# Chapter 2.10
# The Erosive Effect of Not Advertising

> **I don't know who you are.**
> **I don't know your company.**
> **I don't know your product.**
> **I don't know what it stands for.**
> **Now, what was it you wanted to sell me?**
> *~Adapted from a famous*
> *McGraw Hill advertisement*

*Synopsis: Readers will be familiar with the theoretical "S" curve for the sales of a new brand establishing itself. They will also have a sense of a "Reverse S" when a brand is allowed to decline. For understandable reasons, though, companies have not invested in researching what happens when they remove advertising support. A UK study, spanning 26 years, throws light on this.*

An airliner, once it reaches cruising altitude, can switch off its engines and glide for a while (even gracefully at first) before gravity takes its toll. This exemplifies the Brand Paradox:

Because of Brand Equity a brand does not immediately crash if it is under-supported.

This creates considerable temptation to pull investment from the brand.

**Figure 2.10 – 1. The Brand Paradox**

It's ironic. Advertising helps brands get to a good altitude. But if you cut support they don't come spiralling out of the sky. This leads to a familiar scenario: the company needs to hit its financial targets, and the advertising budget goes helplessly to the chopping block.

Stephan Buck, in his paper, "The True Cost of Cutting Adspend," has evidence that may blunt the hatchets. He states that:

> Advertising support, in general, is causally related to long-term brand health—and the lack of it causes brands to suffer.

The story is worth telling in some detail.

Dr. Buck, through the leading UK research firm Taylor Nelson Sofres, got access to valid, comparable packaged goods data for twenty six years: 1975 through 2001. This history could be broken into two eras, divided by the watershed year of 1997.

In the first era, UK supermarkets aggressively built their private label business. At the same time the leading packaged goods brands were, in general, well supported by advertising.

In the second era, the supermarkets took the focus off private label (which would help advertised brands), but a new pressure arrived—Everyday Low Prices. Over this period, the advertised brands reduced their spending in real terms. This allowed Dr. Buck to examine what happened in the two very different advertising environments.

**1975–1997.** Private Label share almost doubled. It went from 16 to 30 points, putting a lot of pressure on manufacturer brands. The bigger (advertised) brands, however, did comparatively well. It was the small (largely unadvertised) brands that took the brunt of the losses.

| (Excludes Private Label) | 1975 | 1997 |
|---|---|---|
| Number 1 brand | 40.9 | 45.5 |
| Number 2 brand | 18.3 | 19.6 |
| Tertiary brands (> 2% share) | 23.0 | 22.7 |
| Other Brands (< 2% share) | 17.7 | 12.2 |

**Table 2.10 – 2. Average Share Structure amongst Branded Goods**
Source: The True Cost of Cutting Adspend. warc.com (2002)

Dr. Buck took the #1 and #2 brands, and ranked them as Winners or Losers, according to share performance. He then related Winners and Losers to adspend, and found a strong correlation between heavier adspend and marketplace success:

| (Constant prices: 1975 = 100) | | |
| --- | --- | --- |
| | 1975 | 1997 |
| Winners | 100 | 241 |
| Losers | 100 | 162 |

**Table 2.10 – 3. Changes in Average Adspend for Long-Term Winners and Losers**
Source: The True Cost of Cutting Adspend. warc.com (2002)

He also found that higher spend tended to precede success, suggesting cause and effect.

**The Watershed Year—1997.** This is when the government got interested in supermarket pricing, and the supermarkets and manufacturers responded with Everyday Low Prices (EDLP). This had to be paid for, of course.

The plan was that supermarkets would cut back on weekly specials (which are ultimately funded by manufacturers). Perhaps we shouldn't be surprised that the cuts never occurred. Or that manufacturers, by 2001, had cut adspend by 19% in real terms. On the positive side, though, supermarkets put less into Private Label, and by 2001 PL share had fallen from 30 points to 26 points.

**1997–2001.** This led to a surprise.

| (Excludes Private Label) | | |
| --- | --- | --- |
| | 1997 | 2001 |
| Number 1 brand | 45.5 | 44.7 |
| Number 2 brand | 19.6 | 20.0 |
| Tertiary brands (> 2% share) | 22.7 | 26.0 |
| Other Brands (< 2% share) | 12.2 | 9.3 |

**Table 2.10 – 4. Average Share Structure amongst Branded Goods**
Source: The True Cost of Cutting Adspend. warc.com (2002)

The leading brands had done comparatively well when Private Label was forging ahead, and so could be expected to do well when this pressure was taken off. But it didn't happen. The very small brands continued to suffer, but (as noted in Table 2.10 – 3) the tertiary brands responded the best.

The explanation traced to ad spending. It's complicated by the fact that EDLP forced all ad spending down, but the pattern is clear from the following graph, which is reproduced from Dr. Buck's paper. It shows that the Losers were the brands with the steep advertising cuts:

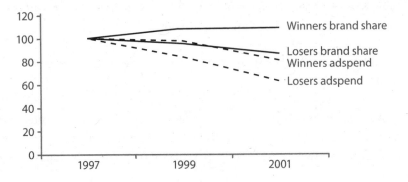

**Figure 2.10 – 5. Winners vs. Losers (1997–2001)**
Source: The True Cost of Cutting Adspend. warc.com (2002)

Separately, Dr. Buck analysed share patterns for the three UK recessions that occurred during 1975–2001. He found a clear correlation between adspend and subsequent success. And speaking to his overall conclusions, he says:

> *These results strongly suggest that relatively heavy and continuous advertising is a causal factor in premium brands achieving success in both the short and long term, even in a commercially difficult environment.*

This is in line with the findings from Pepper, Butterfield, BehaviorScan, and Hess and Ambach. So perhaps Messrs. Lever and Wanamaker are resting a bit easier now.

# Chapter 2.11
# The Value of Marketing

> **A cynic knows the cost of everything and the value of nothing.**
>
> ~*Oscar Wilde*

Marketing, like other terms in business, has many meanings. At one end of the spectrum there is the revered legacy of Theodore Levitt and Peter Drucker. These and other top thinkers have transformed business by altering the entire strategic framework.

At the other end—particularly from a Finance point of view—there's a sense that marketing is just a tactical and even gimmicky way to push sales.

Levitt and Drucker would be astonished to see the value of marketing being called in question. And we hope this book has helped put it in its rightful place. We also thought it would be useful to collect our main references to academic work in a single chapter.

Research into marketing and *business value* has, until recently, been limited. For many years the interest leant more towards the social science side.

A notable exception came in 1994, when David Aaker and Robert Jacobson published "The Financial Information Content of Perceived Quality" in the Journal of Marketing Research. This demonstrated that the movement in stock prices could be better explained by reference to changes in ROI and Brand Equity (the latter defined as "perceived product quality" and measured using EquiTrend data) than by changes in ROI alone.

The next milestone was in the late 1990s with work by Rajendra Srivastava, Tassaduk Shervani and Liam Fahey—in particular "Market-Based Assets and Shareholder Value" published in the Journal of Marketing in 1998. They showed that "soft" assets like Brand Equity and Customer/Trade Relationships could be looked at through a "hard" financial filter. This started to create a bridge between Finance and Marketing, with common language for assessing the financial importance of marketing assets.

Meanwhile, Tom Madden at the Moore School of Business (University of South Carolina), Frank Fehle at Barclays Global Investors, and Susan Fournier of the Tuck School at Dartmouth, were pursuing another line of enquiry. "Brands Matter—An Empirical Investigation of Brand Building and the Creation of Shareholder Value" was published in 2006 in the Journal of the Academy of Marketing Science.

As noted in Chapter 1.9, this compared the long-term stock market performance of two portfolios. One consisted of 100+ highly branded companies. The other was the Russell 3000, essentially the whole market. The highly branded companies significantly outperformed the market for August 1994 through December 2000.

To Finance, this study is intriguing as it flies in the face of financial ortho-doxy—which maintains that you cannot enjoy superior financial returns without assuming additional risk (an observation for which William Sharpe won the Nobel Prize in Economics in 1990 and which, through the work of Eugene Fama and Kenneth French, has evolved into the foundation for mod-ern portfolio theory). Yet these findings suggest that strong brands permit companies to deliver superior earnings and at lower risk.

Related work was also being done by BrandEconomics.[33] They had the BrandAsset® Valuator (BAV) database, developed and maintained by the Corporate Research Group at Young & Rubicam. They also had the Economic Value Added (EVA®) database developed and maintained by Stern Stewart. They could look at companies with different valuation multiples, and see if brand health could help explain the differences. They found, not unexpect-edly, that profitability (returns above the cost of capital) explained some 50% of the variance. But they found that they could account for up to 80% of the variance in company valuations if they also added a metric for brand strength to their valuation model.

Finally, Natalie Mizik of the Columbia Business School and Robert Jacobson at the University of Washington Business School were using BrandAsset® Valuator (BAV) in a different way. They took 275 monobrand companies (companies doing their business essentially under a single brand name) and compared stock performance to brand health.

---

33 See Bergesen, M. and Ehrbar, A., "A New Approach to Managing Brand and Business Value," Institutional Investor Journals, November 2002.

They found a direct relationship between perceived levels of brand differentiation and the level of stock returns one year later. They also isolated the metrics most strongly related to improvements in current earnings (quality, familiarity and differentiation), and those most predictive of future earnings (relevance and vitality). They established a powerful rule of thumb—that when brand health changes, one third of the impact shows up in current earnings, and two thirds in future earnings.

All of this gives Marketing, and by implication Advertising, distinct financial credentials, and it brings us to the end of Part 2. We'll now review what we have covered.

# Key Points from Part 2

- For brands to be successful, they need to go beyond product and win the hearts and minds of consumers, using the "moreness" that appeals to Earthlings.
- In an ideal world, we would see a growth in short-term earnings *and* an increase in Brand Equity. The real world often requires a trade-off between short-term and long-term results.
- There is an understandable tendency for these decisions to be influenced by the Immediacy Effect and the Measurability Effect. Though it involves judgment calls, it would be better to be guided by finding the best balance between the short and long term.
- The Lever/Wannamaker "half my advertising" quote is proverbially popular, but it is misleading.
- Effective advertising has a short-term effect, though this can be masked by other tactics, e.g., promotion, price, distribution etc.
- Several sources show that advertising has a long-term effect that is double or more the short-term effect.
- Long-term research in the UK packaged goods industry also shows that there is a noticeable business cost to cutting adspend.
- Academic research on a number of fronts confirms the business value of marketing effort, and by implication advertising.
- All this suggests that it's time for closer co-operation between Finance, Marketing and Advertising.

### End of Part 2

# PART 3

# CREATING A SHARED
# ACCOUNTABILITY CULTURE

In Part 1, we saw that Brand Equity represents the "moreness" of a successful brand, delivering superior cash flow now and over time. This gives Finance, Marketing and Advertising a common interest in creating and nurturing strong brands.

In Part 2, we explored how strong brands win the battle for the customer's heart and mind by augmenting functional Vulcan benefits with psychological Earthling appeal. We saw evidence for the long term impact of advertising—with various sources showing that this is often greater than the short term impact—supporting the notion that strong brands are "reservoirs of future cash flow."

In Part 3 we shift gears, to deal with the question, *"What do we do?"*

This is a fluid topic. There are different ideas as to what Accountability entails. For some it's an ROI calculation (with varying meanings of ROI). For others it's the output of a Marketing Mix Model. Some think in terms of formal Brand Valuation. Others look to Marketing Dashboards and Brand Scorecards. All capture the impact of marketing and advertising in their own way, but none of them give the complete answer.

Various companies and experts have published what they've learned as they've hacked their way through the undergrowth of possibilities, and we can add our experience to that. The overarching learning is that an Accountability Culture is mandatory. *Attitude, intent and co-operation* are essential, and without them the results of any approach will be disappointing.

Overall, companies are at different levels of creating this culture. But once Marketing and Advertising think of their activities in business terms, and Finance take an active interest in Brand Equity, there's a dramatic improvement in Accountability, and the corresponding business results.

# Chapter 3.1
# The Need for Teamwork—Led from the Top

> **They're not so much a team. More a loose confederation of warring tribes.**
> *~The UK Cabinet, described in "Yes Prime Minister," a British political sitcom*

All sources—and this is in line with our experience—say that to create an Accountability Culture you need a cross-functional team led from the top. The leader should come at least from the Senior VP level, and the CEO should be visibly involved. The priority question is, "Are we getting an appropriate return, short and long term, on our marketing and advertising dollar?" Other questions also have to be asked:

- Who should be on the Accountability team?
- What is the right way to look at return?[1]
- Do we have a Causal Model, and are the metrics aligned to corporate objectives?
- What is a reasonable time to get a system de-bugged and up and running?
- How will turf problems be handled?
- Will the outputs be available in time to be actionable?
- Will the system account for short- and long-term factors?
- Who ensures the integrity of the data?
- Who reports and interprets the results?
- Will the reported results be easy to interpret and understand?[2]
- Will the system be able to predict future performance, or will it just explain the past?
- In the zeal to measure, will creativity be damaged or destroyed?
- What will it cost? Is it worth the time, effort, and culture-shock?

There's no cookie-cutter answer, and as can be seen, it's not a quick fix. It takes serious, dedicated, long-term commitment.

---

1 This relates to the "ROI" question in Chapter 1.1.
2 This is a reference to Marketing Dashboards and Brand Scorecards. See Chapter 3.12.

# Chapter 3.2
# Measurability

> **You can't manage what you can't measure.**
> *~Peter Drucker*

> **Not everything that can be measured matters.**
> **Not everything that matters can be measured.**
> *~Albert Einstein*

Given that Drucker and Einstein don't agree, it's not surprising that there are squabbles over measurability. Business usually favours Drucker.[3] But it's worth bearing in mind that measurement is not the exact science it purports to be.

In ancient Rome, they read the entrails of chickens. We laugh now, but in the boardrooms of the day it was a respected research technique. Paul Feldwick, in one of his papers, notes how today's quantitative ad researchers "stress the merits of their particular method with a bewildering degree of conviction."

Along the same lines, the economist Robert Chambers warns against the tyranny of numbers saying, "Quantification brings credibility, but figures and tables can deceive, and numbers construct their own realities."

There will always be Vulcan-Earthling dissonance. Agencies, especially creative people, are regarded with suspicion when they resist the slide-rule. But how do you measure an idea? Some famously successful business leaders have dismissed traditional research, relying on experience and judgment for major decisions.[4] Even P&G, renowned for its analytical discipline, had the maxim, "It's better to do no research than bad research."

So, when designing a system of Accountability, make sure that clumsy measurement or inappropriate timeframes do not kill good ideas.

---

3  However, consider the resurgence of Design, which is now being elevated to the level of business strategy. Design takes the Einsteinian view of measurability.
4  Phil Knight of Nike, Richard Branson of Virgin, Howard Schultz of Starbucks and Steve Jobs of Apple come to mind.

# Chapter 3.3
# The "Now and Later" Mindset

> **The future has a habit of arriving.**
> ~Strategic Planner's maxim

A "Now and Later" Mindset needs to be encouraged because some people focus too much on the short-term, and some do the opposite. The need for immediate results is obvious. But equally, brands must be nurtured.

In Chapter 2.9 we saw that a brand's baseline sales are often the biggest contributor to the business by far, and those sales are caused by accumulated Brand Equity. *So when we undermine Brand Equity, we put at risk the biggest single contributor to future sales.* As a result, a marketing plan must be balanced—and we can represent this as an evolution of to the Two-Fold Measurement diagram in Chapter 1.1:

**Figure 3.3 – 1. The "Now and Later" Mindset**

It has to be said, though, that people frequently regress to their overly short- or long-term view, and we'll comment on this.

### Why the Short-Term View Alone is Not Enough
Some effort delivers results in the short term, but with potentially damaging effects long term.[5]

---

5  The Employee Pricing wars in Chapter 2.4 are a spectacular example of "training consumers to expect a price cut."

Paul Feldwick also makes an analogy to physical exercise. Sporadic effort does not have much benefit. But a co-ordinated programme, designed with long-term goals in mind, can make a big difference.[6]

### Why the Long-Term View Alone is Not Enough

Another analogy. Toronto is trying to deal with guns and violence. The long-term thinkers say that we have to deal with the underlying social issues. They are right, but this will not be enough for a comprehensive plan, because the results will come in far too slowly. Like a classic marketing plan, the problem needs short- *and* long-term results.

To misquote Fram air filters, "You have to deliver now, *and* you have to deliver later."

---

6 There are milking situations where the short-term view is right. But even the most diehard short termer knows that this is not the right strategy for brands with long-term potential.

# Chapter 3.4
# Defining the Causal Model

> **If you don't know where you are going,**
> **any road will get you there.**
> ~*The Cheshire Cat in* Alice in Wonderland

We started Part 1 with a long quote from David Aaker. It closed with these words:

> *The rationale for investment in any intangible asset [e.g. a brand] must rest in part on a conceptual model of the business that is often not easy to generate or defend. Without such a model, though, movement towards brand leadership is inhibited.*

Then, in Chapter 1.7 we said that Finance wanted:

> *Some sort of Causal Model, with identified assumptions, to explain how marketing and advertising effort contributes to business success.*

As the Cheshire Cat would understand, such a Causal Model is "not easy to generate or defend." Despite the academic evidence that brands have great value, no one had found an easily-measured connection between the marketing activity that creates this value and the resulting financial performance. Even so, it is the first big task for the team.

This is quite a challenge for the reasons we've been discussing. But there's good news. The very fact of getting Finance, Marketing and Advertising (and other disciplines) together to decide a Causal Model is *itself* valuable in creating common ground. Marketing and Advertising can show their business mindset, and Finance can get a closer look at what creates the added value of brands.

It has to be said, though, that these discussions can be mind-numbing. Sooner or later someone wonders if there is an off-the-shelf answer.

The short answer is no, because each business is different, and therefore has to identify its own drivers. More generally, though, there are proprietary methodologies (we discuss them later) that can be incorporated into the system.

In terms of benchmarks, organizations like Procter & Gamble and Mastercard have gone public with their experiences. They make it clear that there are no quick fixes, and that the answer lies more in creating an *accountability culture* than in using any particular measurement technique.

Unisys has gone further. They've been altruistic enough to publish a detailed paper of their work. We cover the highlights in Chapter 3.13, and the paper itself is well worth reading.

Finally, we'll re-state the point that the Causal Model must account not only for short-term effects—but also increases or decreases in Brand Equity.

The net of all this is that the company must be prepared to invest considerable time and effort at the "Causal Model" stage. But it is an essential first step, to make sure that all subsequent effort is on a firm and valid foundation.

To illustrate what we mean, the next two chapters profile two possible approaches. The first is based on the Sales Funnel concept. The second is based on the Value Chain concept.

# Chapter 3.5
# The Sales Funnel Model

> **Come into my parlour, said the spider to the fly...**
>
> *~Children's poem*

This model suits the culture of sales-led businesses where a good deal of the marketing and advertising activity is focussed on generating leads—though there is usually a brand-building role too. Insurance, office equipment and B2B technology come to mind.

The model uses the familiar sales-based metrics: the number of prospects entering the funnel; their speed through the sales process; drop out rate; and eventual purchase size and frequency. The goal is to document the changes in these variables that result from an investment in advertising and marketing. Results are then compared to previously observed norms.

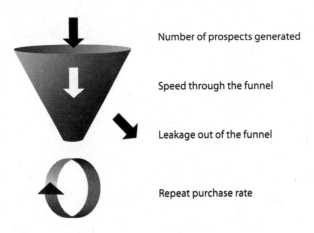

Number of prospects generated

Speed through the funnel

Leakage out of the funnel

Repeat purchase rate

**Figure 3.5 – 1. The Sales Funnel**

With this approach, Marketing and Sales will often have what the diplomats call a "free and frank" exchange of views about their respective contributions to sales performance (and how they might be improved). But overall, in the appropriate businesses, it is an excellent basis for the Causal Model discussion.

# Chapter 3.6
# The Brand Value Chain Model

> **I'm not looking for absolute certainty.**
> **Just a set of testable assumptions.**
>
> ~*Company CFO*

The Brand Value Chain is another way of approaching the Causal Model. Its goal is to map out how cash invested in marketing activity ultimately leads to additional cash (profit) for the company.

This responds to the Finance requirement for treating the brand as a financial asset i.e. they can see a correlation between "what consumers carry in their heads" and behaviour that adds to cash flow. It also works for Marketing and Advertising, because the metrics are based on marketing activities. The specifics of the Value Chain vary by industry, but it essentially has five parts:

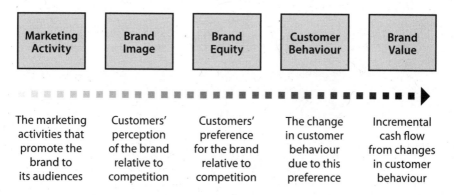

| Marketing Activity | Brand Image | Brand Equity | Customer Behaviour | Brand Value |
|---|---|---|---|---|
| The marketing activities that promote the brand to its audiences | Customers' perception of the brand relative to competition | Customers' preference for the brand relative to competition | The change in customer behaviour due to this preference | Incremental cash flow from changes in customer behaviour |

**Figure 3.6 – 1. The Brand Value Chain**

The assumption is that cash invested in marketing goes through three transformations before it re-emerges as cash in the company's bank account. The first transformaion is into Brand Image—the associations in customers' minds. The second is into Brand Equity—the customer preference this image creates. The third is into the Customer Behaviour that generates incremental cash flow and Brand Value.[7]

---

7  We find it useful to distinguish between Brand Image and Brand Equity. David Aaker and Tim Ambler tend to use "Brand Equity" to cover both meanings. See Chapters 1.10 and 1.11.

Brand Image, Brand Equity and Customer Behaviour are what Finance people call intermediary variables. They are not ends in themselves, but they are predictive of cash flow that will ultimately be generated.

It's therefore important to have key metrics for them. Each will give an indication—with varying degrees of lag—about the future performance of the business. Changes in Customer Behaviour give immediate insight into changes in revenue, while Brand Equity and Brand Image give insight into brand health, and hence the longer term prospects for the business.

It's also important for everyone to accept that there are few if any pre-set formulas for nailing down cause and effect. The Accountability team has to agree on the likely key business drivers; measure them; correlate this to actual business performance; and continuously refine the model as more information comes in.

That said, the literature is full of suggestions as to the metrics that are usually the most important, and that's our next topic.

# Chapter 3.7
# What to Measure

> **If it moves, salute it. If it doesn't move, pick it up. If you can't pick it up, paint it.**
> ~Advice to Army Recruits

There's a habit, especially in big companies, to over-measure. Masses of data gather dust in different departments, with no one having the time (or inclination) to turn information into usable knowledge. To avoid this:

- Identify Key Drivers—influencing the short and long term.
- Focus on the 20 percent of drivers that deliver 80 percent of the business.
- Keep the number of metrics manageable.[8]
- Make sure they are measured in a way that is above reproach.
- Find a succinct, visual, updatable way to present the findings, keeping top management particularly in mind.
- Capture "second-level" diagnostics, but don't let them clutter the system. Make them accessible by drilling down.

Each company should make its own decisions, but here's a summary of commonly recommended metrics:

| David Aaker | Tim Ambler | Alan Middleton |
|---|---|---|
| Price Premium | Relative Satisfaction | *Aaker's List, plus* |
| Satisfaction/Loyalty | Commitment/Loyalty | Share of Requirements |
| Perceived Quality | Relative Perceived Quality | Lifetime Value of a Customer |
| Leadership/Popularity | Relative Price | |
| Perceived Value/ | Availability | |
|   Differentiation | Sales/Market Share | **Rutherford/Knowles** |
| Brand Personality | Marketing Investment | |
| Organizational Associations | Profit | *The other selections, plus* |
| Brand Awareness | Innovation | Willingness to Pay a Premium |
| Market Share | Employee Satisfaction etc. | Willingness to Recommend |
| Price/Distribution | | Relevant Differentiation |

**Figure 3.7 – 1. Variables to Measure (vs. Objectives and Competition)**

---

8 The general advice puts twenty or so as the upper limit, though some companies have managed to design systems that accommodate more.

Other suggestions come from Kevin Lane Keller, the Professor of Marketing at the Tuck School at Dartmouth and co-author with Philip Kotler of *Marketing Management*. He does not define specific metrics, but has invaluable advice for what drives brands:

- The brand excels at delivering the benefits customers truly desire.
- The brand stays relevant.
- The pricing strategy is based on consumers' perceptions of value.
- The brand is properly positioned.
- The brand is consistent.
- The brand portfolio and hierarchy make sense.
- The brand makes use of and coordinates a full repertoire of marketing activities to build equity.
- The brand managers understand what the brand means to consumers.
- The brand is given proper support, and that support is sustained over the long run.
- The company monitors sources of brand equity.

Source: The Brand Report Card, *Harvard Business Review*. Jan./Feb. 2000.

Many of the metrics that are eventually chosen affect the Brand Value Chain, so we'll now look at that in more detail.

# Chapter 3.8
# Drilling Down

> **God is in the details.**
> *~Mies van der Rohe*

As we've noted, the effect of some marketing activity (e.g. Direct Response and the Internet) is relatively easy to measure. Assuming it qualifies as a Key Driver, it can be incorporated without much difficulty into an Accountability system.

Other activity (advertising, product placement, sponsorship, PR, most buzz effort) is more complicated. Depending on priorities, two different approaches may be suitable. Market Mix Modeling may be right if your goal is to understand the short term sales impact of various marketing tactics. However, if you want to identify the aggregate benefit of your marketing investment, the Brand Value Chain from Chapter 3.6 is a powerful organizing framework.

It appeals to those with a "logic and reason" world view because it offers a coherent, sequential view of how marketing/advertising effort is impacting business performance and value:

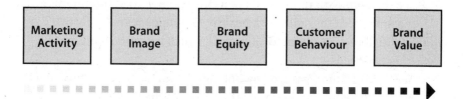

**Figure 3.8 – 1. The Brand Value Chain**

There are a number of measurement techniques associated with each step, and they can be used to diagnose a brand's situation and progress. Perceptual Maps show the image that customers have of a brand; Brand Equity Models measure the nature and scale of preference; Customer Utility Models explain purchase behaviour in terms of Vulcan and Earthling appeals; and Brand Value Models complete the picture. We'll comment briefly on each.

## Marketing Mix Modelling

This is an econometric technique for assessing the optimal allocation of marketing spending across different activities. It is based on detailed historical data, and uses complex mathematics to show which tactics are working, and to what degree. Sir Martin Sorrell went so far as to refer to econometrics as "the holy grail of advertising" in 2005. However, the euphoria needs to be tempered by three considerations:

- The models, as noted, are short term in their focus—and do not fully account for the contribution of Brand Equity.[9]
- They are voracious in their appetite for data. This means that they can rarely be used outside of high transaction environments such as consumer packaged goods.
- They are not suited to rapidly changing markets. Their predictions are purely extrapolations of the past.

## Perceptual Maps

These generate a two-dimensional picture of how customers "see" competing brands. They work by generating statistical correlations. For example, in Correspondence Maps, attributes where brands score equally well (or equally poorly) plot close to the centre. Attributes with a wide variance plot away from the centre. At a glance, the maps allow you to:

- See the dominant dimensions that divide the market (premium to mass; modern to traditional; healthy to indulgent and so forth).
- See attributes common to all brands, which therefore represent category needs.
- See the attributes "owned" by individual brands, thereby throwing light on how they are winning the battle for the heart and mind.

## Brand Equity Models

These sit at the midpoint between "cash invested" and "cash generated," and are often the single most important tool in Accountability. In view of this, we've devoted the next chapter to profiling some of the more insightful approaches.

---

9  See Chapter 1.23.

## Customer Utility Models

These include such methods as Conjoint Analysis and Structured Equation Modelling. They are broadly similar to Marketing Mix Models—expressing customer preference (or utility) in terms of the contribution made by individual product features.

They work by asking customers to express their relative preference for a range of product offerings, each with multiple features and benefits. Customers rank alternatives in descending order of preference. From this, the model can infer the utility associated with each component (bottle vs. box, powder vs. liquid, blue vs. red, two-for-one vs. price reduction). This can be particularly useful for pricing decisions because it suggests the price premium or discount that is appropriate for a given overall utility score.

## Brand Value Models

These put a dollar value on brands or marketing activities by identifying the incremental cash flows earned as a result of the strength of the brand or the effectiveness of the effort. They are aiming to deliver an ROI measurement (in the true sense given in Chapter 1.1) although this is more often expressed as a Net Present Value figure.

As with Brand Equity, this topic merits a dedicated chapter. Actually two. Chapter 3.10 describes when a formal brand valuation is required (not as often as you might think). Chapter 3.11 describes how to do it.

# Chapter 3.9
# Measuring Brand Equity

> **How do I love thee? Let me count the ways.**
> *~Elizabeth Barrett Browning*

We measure Brand Equity so as to have reliable data that money invested in marketing is building an asset that will generate cash flow in the future. Note both requirements. Brand Equity needs to tie back to marketing activity, and forward to cash flow. It's perhaps not surprising that measurement techniques tend to fulfill one requirement more satisfactorily than the other.

In fact, there are two camps. Both measure the preference that a brand enjoys. The first tends to tie forwards—emphasizing intention, behaviour and cash flow. The second ties back—focussing on the sources of "moreness," and Relevant Differentiation.[10]

Fred Reichheld is a proponent of the first camp. He is the author of *The Loyalty Effect* and *Loyalty Rules!* His premise is simple, that "willingness to recommend to a friend" is the single most reliable measure of Brand Equity. He proposes that the "net promoter" score (the number of people willing to recommend a brand minus those who are not) is an accurate predictor of the brand's growth prospects. This is radically simple. He suggests that this one metric can replace a whole battery of attitudinal and behavioural questions that appear in most research questionnaires.

In similar vein is the idea that "willingness to pay a price premium" (and actually doing so) is the acid test. This approach is popular because it gives input to valuation models. Professor Don Lehmann of Columbia University advocates a "revenue premium" method. It measures the value of a brand versus a generic alternative by looking at the incremental revenue it generates through enhanced volume or price premium.

---

10 Note that we are not endorsing or de-endorsing any approach.

These approaches are useful, but they can be limited for two reasons:

- Consumers tend to overstate their intentions, and their willingness to change how they behave.
- They provide limited insight into what is creating Brand Equity.

The second camp is concerned with the source and scale of Brand Equity, and we'll now summarize six approaches.

**Equity Engine™**

This is the methodology developed by Research International, a leading market research firm.

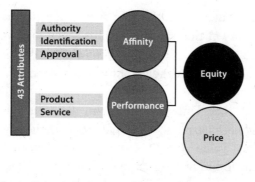

**Figure 3.9 – 1. Property of Research International**

It measures customer perceptions on three dimensions—Price, Functional Performance, and Affinity (or Emotional Performance). Functional Performance is driven by what is seen to be a credible offering in the category. Affinity captures the emotional and intangible attributes that customers associate with the brand. These include Identification (the closeness customers feel to the brand), Approval (the status the brand enjoys) and Authority (the reputation of the brand).

Functional Performance and Affinity together determine Brand Equity. The purchase decision can then be examined, to see how much it is influenced by Brand Equity and Price. In essence, Equity Engine™ establishes the price premium that a brand's equity will support while still maintaining a "good value for money" rating from customers.

## BrandAsset® Valuator

This is the methodology developed by Young & Rubicam, a leading advertising agency.

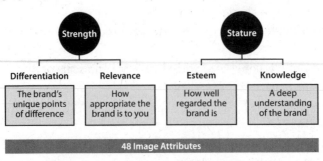

**Figure 3 .9 – 2. Property of Young & Rubicam**

The BrandAsset® Valuator (BAV) is a worldwide database that measures the customer equity of thousands of brands along four main dimensions—Differentiation, Relevance, Esteem and Knowledge. BAV is unique in that it measures brand equity independent of category context.

Y&R discovered that Differentiation and Relevance can be combined to form Brand Strength, a construct that is highly correlated with superior market value (see Chapter 2.11). Esteem and Knowledge combine to form Brand Stature—a metric that correlates closely to current market share.

## Equity*Builder™

This is the methodology developed by the Ipsos Group, another leading market research firm.

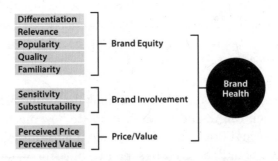

**Figure 3.9 – 3. Property of Ipsos Group**

Equity*Builder™ delivers an overall brand health score based on three components—a brand's attitudinal equity, the customer involvement with the category, and price/value perceptions. The scores are based on a number of individual elements – for example, attitudinal equity is the composite of familiarity, perceived uniqueness, relevance, popularity and quality.

**BrandDynamics™**
This is the methodology proposed by Millward Brown, another leading market research firm.

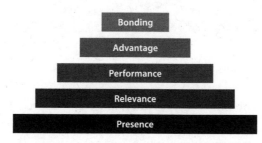

**Figure 3.9 – 4. Property of Millward Brown**

BrandDynamics™ segments a company's customer base according to attachment to the brand, with five levels of attachment—Presence, Relevance, Performance, Advantage and Bonding. "Presence" customers have only a basic awareness of the brand. The attachment increases through the other levels, with "Bonded" customers being intensely loyal—often acting as advocates for the brand in question.

This is a powerful methodology for mapping the loyalty distribution of a brand's customer base, and where to focus in order to shift customers to higher levels of loyalty.

The brand's loyalty profile can be expressed as a single Brand Voltage™ number that indicates likely success in migrating customers up the pyramid. This number is a strong predictor of a brand's potential to grow.

## Kevin Lane Keller's Brand Resonance Model

Although not available as a commercial methodology, this model is worth mentioning because of Keller's authority in the brand equity arena.

**Figure 3.9 – 5. Property of Kevin Lane Keller**

Keller's model combines the Equity Engine™ approach of expressing brand equity in terms of its rational and emotional components with the BrandDynamics™ approach of using a "pyramid of engagement" to express the level of customer involvement with the brand. It is a helpful framework for measuring the depth of customer engagement and the extent to which the relationship is rationally-dominant or emotionally-dominant.

## Winning B®ands

This is the methodology developed by ACNielsen.

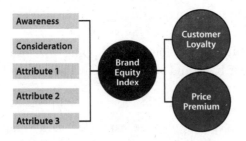

**Figure 3.9 – 6. Property of ACNielsen**

In contrast to the attitudinal approach embodied in other approaches, Winning B®ands begins from a behavioural observation of brand equity. It is measured in terms of a customer's frequency of purchase and the price premium paid. Having established this favourable behaviour, the methodology seeks to analyze the attitudinal characteristics of those customers.

In this sense, Winning Brands is closest in philosophy to the Reichheld and Lehmann approaches mentioned at the start of this chapter.

Each of these models has its merits and serves to provide insight into the "moreness" of a brand and the depth of the reservoir of goodwill that the brand has created. This leads naturally to the question about the valuation of this reservoir, and that's where we go next.

# Chapter 3.10
# Brand Valuation—When to Do It

> **[He] who steals my purse steals trash...**
> **But he that filches from me my good name...**
> **makes me poor indeed.**
>
> ~*William Shakespeare*

The Interbrand and Millward Brown league tables (see Chapter 1.9) have raised awareness of the financial significance of having a good name. But Brand Valuation is not the silver bullet of Accountability. As Aaker has pointed out:

> *The value of a brand cannot be estimated precisely...such estimates cannot be used to evaluate marketing programmes.*[11]

That said, there is still a use for Brand Valuation. In fact, three uses:

- Accounting purposes.
- Helping decide the terms of a prospective transaction.
- Enhancing the management of the brand.

## *Accounting Purposes*

The US and international accounting standards (Financial Accounting Standard 141 and International Financial Reporting Standard 3) require that "goodwill" in an acquisition (the excess of the purchase price over the value of the tangible assets acquired) be allocated to the intangible assets that the company is acquiring.

In Chapter 1.13, we reviewed the five classes of intangible assets suggested by the International Accounting Standards Board, noting that brands fall within the category of "marketing-related assets" for accounting purposes.

This means that the valuation of marketing-related assets is now part of the due diligence performed before an acquisition.

---

11 From "The Value of the Brand" in Aaker's Brand Leadership.

## Prospective Transactions

There are four categories—securitization, tax-planning, licensing and sale.

*Securitization* involves raising funds against the security of future revenues. David Bowie did this in 1997 by issuing $US55 million of bonds backed by the future royalties on his pre-1990 recordings. Despite a lot of discussion, however, brands have rarely been used as collateral for asset-backed securities, although Sears have recently experimented with issuing bonds backed by the Kenmore, Craftsman and DieHard brands.

*Brand-based tax planning* is, by contrast, relatively common. It involves transferring ownership of the trademark (and usually other forms of intellectual property) to a central holding company—that then charges a royalty to the operating companies for the use of these assets. This not only enhances the management of these assets; it also shields some of the profits of the operating companies from local taxes.

*Brand licensing* requires an understanding of the economic benefit provided by the brand in order to establish an appropriate royalty rate.

*Brand sale* also requires a valuation of the economic benefit provided by the brand, this time expressed as an overall value rather than as a royalty rate.

## Management of the Brand

Here, Brand Valuation can have many benefits, but we also urge caution. A valuation for accounting purposes will use a narrow definition of "brand" as the intellectual property represented by the trademark and associated goodwill. A marketing valuation, on the other hand, will reflect the fact that a brand is "a bundle of meanings," and be based on a broader set of assumptions. It will also not generally be subject to external third-party validation.

This can raise Vulcan-Earthling differences over the business significance of a specific "brand value" number, but this misses the larger point. The *valuation process* forces the company to examine what truly drives success, and this often uncovers brand and business building insights that would otherwise stay undiscovered.

# Chapter 3.11
# Brand Valuation—How to Do It

> **Give us the tools, and we will finish the job.**
> ~*Winston Churchill, referring*
> *to his plans for fighting WWII*

This chapter assumes that you need a Brand Valuation. The goal now is to identify the method of valuation.

For Accounting purposes, there are "historical cost" and "replacement cost" approaches, but we do not need to concern ourselves with them because they measure the historical value of a brand (what it cost to create) as opposed to the value it will generate in future. We are interested in what is known as Economic Use. This establishes the economic benefit that accrues to the brand owner as a result of the brand.

Within Economic Use there are two approaches: Relief from Royalty and Earnings Split.

### *The Relief from Royalty Approach*
This imagines that a business does not own its trademarks but licenses them from another business at a market rate. Under this method, brand value is the net present value of the royalty payments made.

This is the valuation methodology favoured by the fiscal authorities and the courts because it calculates brand value by reference to documented, third-party transactions involving brands of equivalent strength in equivalent industries.

### *The Earnings Split Approach*
Here, the earnings above a break-even economic return on the tangible assets of the business are attributed to the intangible assets. The brand proportion of these intangible earnings is then estimated, generating a stream of earnings attributable to the brand.

This is the approach most commonly used for most marketing purposes e.g. it is the Interbrand and Millward Brown methodology.

There are five major components to the Earnings Split process:

1. *Market and Competitive Context.* This identifies the overall dynamics of the market and the strength of competition.
2. *Business Segmentation.* Brand influence varies by line of business, customer and product type. Consequently, this step divides the business into segments, based on the role played by the brand.
3. *Financial Forecasts.* These are projections for the future earnings of each segment in the previous step.
4. *Brand Value Added.* This involves identifying the drivers of purchase decisions in each segment, and the impact exerted by the brand. The composite brand score across all drivers provides the proportion of total branded business earnings that can be attributed to the brand.
5. *Risk Analysis.* This assesses the strength of the brand's franchise with trade customers and end consumers to establish the security of future brand earnings. The result is a discount rate for the stream of earnings attributable to the brand.

In theory, the two forms of Economic Use should give rise to approximately similar valuations. In practice, the Earnings Split approach tends to produce higher values because it is generally based on a broader definition of brand, and because it allows for growth into new segments.

Typically, therefore, companies end up with two valuations:

- A narrow valuation of the trademark and associated goodwill using Relief from Royalty. This is used to support internal transfer pricing arrangements.
- A marketing valuation using Earnings Split. This demonstrates the overall contribution of the brand to the value of the company.

# Chapter 3.12
# Scorecards and Dashboards

> **They measure what matters, for people who matter.**
>
> ~*Chief Marketing Officer*

In Chapter 2.3, we talked about the Iceberg Challenge. Brands, below the surface, are extraordinarily complex. But what customers see—above the waterline—has to be utterly simple. Accountability is much the same. As an entire field, it's huge. But for Senior Management the measurement system has to be simple.

Marketing Dashboards and Brand Scorecards are still, relatively speaking, in their infancy—but a Google search turned up two and a half million hits for one and a million for the other. So there's a lot of interest.

We can't hope to cover everything, but there are three points worth making.

The first is to explain why we've taken until now to bring up dashboards at all. It's to offset the temptation to get going without (a) setting up a well-led cross-functional team and (b) thinking the project through. If ever there was a danger of Garbage In, Garbage Out, it's by diving in unprepared.

As to Dashboards and Scorecards themselves, the terms are sometimes used interchangeably, but it's useful to keep them separate:

- *Marketing Dashboard.* This "puts the most insightful dials and digits in front of you in a package that's simple, informative and illuminating—all at a glance."[12]
- *Brand Scorecard.* This is part of the Dashboard, with dials and digits that focus on *brand* metrics.

---

12 From Pat LaPointe's *Marketing by the Dashboard Light.*

When it comes to the relative importance of short-term and long-term metrics, these will vary according to the sales cycle and nature of the business, but any measurement system should include some of each. In other words, the approach should match up with the Two-Fold Measurement diagram on page 3.

Finally, Marketing Dashboards and Brand Scorecards should be developed with three specific goals in mind:

- To communicate how marketing and advertising are adding value to the business.
- To monitor progress on key dimensions.
- To focus Senior Management attention on problems and opportunities.

As such, Marketing Dashboards and Brand Scorecards are a philosophical extension of Kaplan and Norton's Balanced Scorecard. This is based on the idea that a financial view of business, though clearly essential, needs to be supplemented by other factors. Their famous diagram follows:

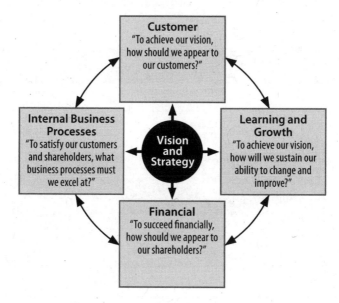

**Figure 3.12 – 1. The Balanced Scorecard**

Adapted from Kaplan and Norton

Some argue that Marketing Dashboards and Brand Scorecards are just the customer dimension of a Balanced Scorecard—but we believe that there are good reasons for keeping the two systems distinct:

- First, there's a tendency for Balanced Scorecards to focus primarily (if not solely) on internal processes. This generates a culture of incremental improvements in business efficiency rather than a focus on step-change success in the marketplace.
- Second, Balanced Scorecards tend to remain "segmented." They describe performance on four dimensions, but do not explain how action on one dimension impacts the others.

Marketing Dashboards and Brand Scorecards go further. They measure what drives success in the marketplace. And they help show that Marketing and Advertising are in the business of creating an asset for the business—with a direct relationship between the metrics tracked and the short- and long-term performance of the business.

These ambitious goals do not mean that the resulting dashboard has to be unwieldy. The dashboard below was developed by Hilton Hotels, and is an excellent example of clarity and simplicity.

| | | | | | Revenue maximization | | Value proposition | | |
|---|---|---|---|---|---|---|---|---|---|---|
| Rank | Rating | Property | Brand standards compliance | Operational effectiveness (EBITDA) | Room RevPAR | RevPAR index | Guest comment cards | Customer-satisfaction tracking study | Team-member survey | Mystery shopper |
| 1 | 6 | Hotel A | 100% | $20,730 | $123.77 | 123.7 | 6.36 | 6.20 | 60% | 94.91% |
| 2 | 6 | Hotel B | 100% | 8,065 | $73.15 | 106.4 | 6.35 | 6.09 | 75% | 91.32% |
| 3 | 5 | Hotel C | 100% | 2,584 | 101.12 | 103.8 | 6.30 | 6.04 | 81% | 89.84% |
| 37 | 3 | Hotel D | 95% | 16,252 | 93.59 | 99.9 | 5.73 | 5.10 | 69% | 85.31% |
| 51 | 3 | Hotel E | 95% | 3,055 | 68.17 | 94.0 | 6.08 | 5.68 | 67% | 88.67% |

**Sample Marketing Dashboard**

Significantly short of goal    Less than goal    Meets or exceeds goal

RevPAR = Revenue per available room

**Figure 3.12 – 2. The Hilton Dashboard**

The dashboard displays key indicators of the Hilton value proposition, plus key metrics for revenue and profitability. Other metrics monitor whether the hotel is delivering the distinctive "Hilton experience." Colour coding makes it immediately clear where performance falls short of target and therefore where senior management attention needs to be focused.

Needless to say, it takes hard work to get to something this simple (Hilton began the dashboard process in 1997). So, in the next two chapters, we'll review two other examples in more depth.

# Chapter 3.13
# The Unisys Example

| **Good enough is not good enough.** |
| *~Variously attributed* |

Unisys remodelled their entire approach to marketing, and its measurement. The following captures the highlights:[13]

*Overview*
Unisys faced issues that will resonate with a lot of readers:

- *Integration.* Unisys had Global & Regional Marketing, but no consolidated reporting of results.
- *Decentralization.* Budgets were managed in six Marketing Organizations. Each had its own strategies and priorities.
- *Visibility.* There was no central repository for information.
- *Opportunity Cost.* Management couldn't identify inefficiency.
- *Accountability.* They could not evaluate Marketing's performance.

Until the Dashboard project, Unisys had no formal vehicle for measuring the return on marketing investment. Now they have a robust, integrated, real-time, on-line system. It features:

- A common set of Marketing goals and objectives across all business units.
- A report of performance for the six Marketing Organizations.
- Information on a Dashboard for the CEO and Board.
- Immediate input for Marketers, so that they can adjust and improve what they do—before it's too late.
- Clear evidence for Management on the value of marketing.
- Stronger alignment between Marketing and Sales.
- Disciplined decision making, based on robust information.

---

13 See "The Unisys Marketing Dashboard," *Journal of Advertising Research,* September 2004, by Jennifer Cioffi of Venture Communications and Amy Miller of Unisys.

### *Getting the Project Off the Ground*

Marketing had to change how it was seen across the company. This started in 2001 with an initiative called Marketing Excellence Architecture, which re-mapped the Marketing function. Next came the Dashboard project. It was imperative for Senior Management and the Executive Committee to endorse the effort. Business Unit leaders also had to get active participation in the process from Sales, Finance and IT.

### *Required Dashboard Characteristics*

Unisys spans a hundred countries, serving clients in Financial Services, Transportation, Communications, Public Sector and Commercial/Media. To measure the effectiveness of this effort, the Dashboard had to be:

- Aligned to corporate priorities.
- Easy to understand. Easy to run.
- Supported by all key players.
- Quantitative (though some qualitative metrics are included).
- Flexible, i.e. designed to allow for future needs.
- Robust, using best practices from other IT companies.
- Tailored to reflect the company's unique needs.

### *Execution*

This came in three phases: Design, Development and Implementation. Design lasted approximately 6 months, with seven steps:

a) Interviewing more than 25 stakeholders re what to measure, why and how it should be done.
b) Aligning this information with corporate goals in four areas: Financial Results, Customers, Employees and Reputation.
c) Mapping stakeholder versus marketing objectives.
d) Getting agreement that the marketing goals were appropriate.
e) Developing a prototype model.
f) Cross-checking the model with the stakeholders, while drilling down to determine how and when the data would be collected.
g) Completing this stage, adjusting several metrics.

With these modifications, the design phase was approved.

Development lasted approximately one month. It started with the selection of software, with these specifications:

- Six dashboards, one for each Marketing Group, preloaded with four corporate goals, nine marketing goals and 27 objectives.
- An aggregate Dashboard of these six, showing overall achievement for Senior Management.
- A browser-based interface that is secure and easy to use.
- The ability to track individual activities.
- Access to custom reports, for budget allocation, cost per lead etc.
- Security safeguards, given the many internal and external users.

This phase ended with an online prototype for testing and de-bugging.

### Implementation and Results

The Dashboard launched in October 2002, and has been a great success. For the first time, Marketing has the information it needs to make fact-based decisions and to adjust its allocation of resources in the light of timely feedback on what is working versus what is not. The Dashboard also helps ensure that marketing effort is aligned with overall Unisys objectives.

# Chapter 3.14
# Drawing the Strands Together

> **O would some power the giftie gie us, to see ourselves as others see us.**
>
> *~Robert Burns*

Major companies are naturally reluctant to release trade secrets, but we thought it would be useful to build a composite case history based on our experience. We'll call the company Pan-Metric.

Pan-Metric is in a highly competitive market, and although its products and services combine good quality and fair pricing, it does not have a sustainable advantage in any of the major Vulcan areas (e.g. patents, high barriers to competitive entry, unique access to low-price raw materials etc.). There is a general sense in the Pan-Metric C-suite that brand-building effort is needed, but the CEO and CFO need more than the CMO's intuition to convince them.

The company is reasonably marketing oriented, but it does not have an entrenched marketing mindset. Historically, it has relied more on an aggressive sales force to do what it has called marketing—but over the last few years this has not been delivering results to the level needed.

The company knows that it needs a more customer-centric approach, but the CEO (who has a financial background) and the CFO also want an Accountability Culture. They decide to re-vamp their operations, and also their approach to measuring success and failure. This is their story, built around four questions:

*Question One—Does "Brand" Add Enough Value to Justify Investment?*
There was debate about whether the "moreness" of brand equity was worth enough to justify investment. The Head of Sales vociferously pointed out that revenues were clearly more responsive to sales effort than to what he regarded as "ivory tower stuff." He also noted that the competition had very different historical levels of advertising, and it wasn't clear (to him at least) that the ones with the highest spending were enjoying higher levels of profitability.

The Production and Distribution people were non-committal. R&D had a sense that "moreness" was a good idea, though they were never entirely comfortable when the talk went beyond the functional or Vulcan aspect of what Pan-Metric offered.

The CMO, not surprisingly, was convinced that there was considerable upside, though had to agree that her point of view rested more on experience and judgment than hard facts. She got support when she quoted academic studies of brand value, but reluctantly conceded that these described the general case, and might not apply to the specifics of Pan-Metric.

The CEO had foreseen these differences, and had asked the CFO to "take an enlightened view." The CEO did not want compromise for its own sake, but equally did not want people digging in based on their pre-conceptions. With the CFO's guidance everyone agreed that more facts were needed. The Head of Sales muttered about "lies, damn lies, and statistics" but eventually everyone agreed that the company needed a financially-based analysis of Pan-Metric and its competitors.

This analysis asked the question: is the market value for Pan-Metric and its major competitors driven by anything more than profitability?

To address this question, we compared the weighted average of Pan Metric's profits for the last 3 years, expressed as a percentage of sales, against their market value, also expressed as a multiple of sales.

As expected, there was a powerful connection between profitability and value multiples. And reflecting this, Pan-Metric was trading at the lower end.

Surprisingly, though, the companies as a whole did not plot as a single competitive set. Usually, there would be one regression line running from the most profitable company to the least. This time, there were two. Something was causing this difference, and it turned out to be advertising pressure.

At any level of profitability, the companies that consistently advertised had a higher value multiple than those who didn't.[14]

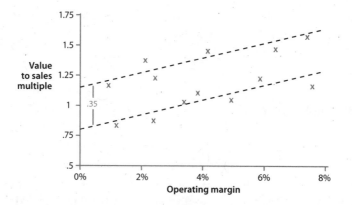

**Figure 3.14 – 1. Margin vs. Value Multiple for Pan-Metric and Competitors**

The difference between the higher and lower line was a valuation multiple of 0.35, making the value of having a strong brand the equivalent of four months' sales. Given annual sales of $US10 billion, this put Pan-Metric's potential brand value at $US3.5 billion. So brand building clearly needed to be investigated further.

### Question Two—Brand Positioning

The focus then shifted to finding the type of positioning that would yield the best return for Pan-Metric. Given the company's low profile, the initial instinct was to emphasize the company's strong credentials on the image attributes that market research showed were most important to customers— in this case, "reliable" and "caring."

Positioning is a huge undertaking. It's beyond our scope to go too deeply into this, but two points are worth mentioning.

---

14 This is in line with the academic findings quoted elsewhere in the book. This pattern would not be so clearly observable in markets where all competitors advertise—though in those markets it is generally agreed that branding is needed; the question is more how to do it than whether to do it.

First, research will often reveal benefits that the company is well placed to deliver.[15] Wonderful! But what if (and it's likely) the competition are equally well placed? Then that seemingly attractive position will be relevant, but not differentiated. This is a dilemma that can be illuminated by techniques such as perceptual mapping (see Chapter 3.8).

Second, we should not forget the inspired intuitive leap that has led to some of the most spectacular positioning decisions of all. (Howard Schultz—how *did* you know that we would pay so much for what Starbucks has to offer?)

In Pan-Metric's case, we used statistical analysis of image research to create a map of how customers saw the industry. Category-wide attributes plotted close to the center. Attributes associated with only a few companies plotted towards the edges. This map allowed the team to see Pan-Metric in a whole new way, and it created huge buy-in. It showed that the initial positioning idea would have been ineffectual, as it would have made Pan-Metric's message indistinguishable from those of its competitors. On the positive side, though, Pan-Metric was distinctive for being "dynamic" and "energetic." This became the basis for a significant positioning shift.

The work also clarified the first step of the Causal Model—what sort of Brand Image the advertising should be aiming to achieve.

### Question Three—How Do We Track Progress?

Considerable thought went into this. There were three questions:

- Should we look for an off-the-shelf solution?
- Which attributes are most important for demonstrating progress?
- Is it possible to create a composite overall Brand Equity score?

The off-the-shelf solution was quickly discarded because it was believed that Pan-Metric's situation was unique.

---

15 To add to the complexity, respondents in research can't always articulate what they want. Henry Ford famously said, "If I'd asked my customers what they wanted, they'd have said a faster horse."

Agreement on "progress" metrics came out of the Causal Model discussion. On the positive side, people saw and understood points of view that they had not considered before. On the other hand, there were tense moments when advocacy was seen as axe-grinding. That was why the CEO had entrusted overall responsibility to a strong and respected leader—one who could bring differing views to a constructive conclusion.

The measurement system needed to satisfy the sales culture and the growing appreciation for Brand Equity. This led to a Marketing Dashboard based on the Sales Funnel approach (see Chapter 3.5) and a Brand Scorecard based on the Brand Value Chain (see Chapters 3.6 and 3.8).

The question of an overall Brand Equity score was challenging. It recognized that senior management had little appetite for tortuous discussion about image and other intermediate attributes. They wanted a single, intuitive metric that demonstrated the level of progress against strategy.

This part of the project needed an understanding that such simplicity may well not be possible. Certainly, people like Tim Ambler have argued that it is an unrealistic expectation. However, we had success.

With some sophisticated mathematics and a lot of iterations we were able to collapse the weighted average scores for key image attributes into a single metric of Differentiated Relevance. Equally important, this metric explained much of the variance of a company's valuation—above what would be expected based on profitability alone.[16]

### Question Four—How Do We Estimate the Value Created?
This question was the final piece of the puzzle. If we could answer it with reasonable precision we would be close to our Accountability goal—showing that investment in marketing and advertising had produced the asset of Brand Equity, with a financial value attractively higher than the investment.

---

16 We don't mean to suggest that this sort of correlation will always be available.

Ironically, this final piece of analysis was the simplest. We had done the work to understand the relationship between the image attributes and the composite metric of Differentiated Relevance. We had also calibrated this metric so that it explained the valuations of competitive companies (adjusted to reflect different levels of profitability).

Given this, it was relatively simple to create an equation that estimated the impact on valuation of an increase in Differentiated Relevance. Once this was known, it was also relatively simple to put an estimated financial value on shifting the perceptions for key image attributes.

Most importantly, it was understood that the valuation was not an end in itself—its goal was to enable better decision-making. Pan-Metric was able to express the investment case for initiatives designed to deliver customer value and build the brand.

### Overall, a Larger Benefit

Historically, Pan-Metric had been reasonably successful, but there had been a substantial lack of alignment in how internal departments and outside suppliers approached the business. As a result of this initiative the sense of shared purpose and mutual respect noticeably improved, as did the financial performance of the company.

# Chapter 3.15
# A Final Word

> **When all is said and done, more will be said than done.**
>
> *~Marshall McLuhan*

We hope Marshall McLuhan is wrong this time. Yes, Accountability takes a great deal of discussion and planning. But concrete results are essential. Here's a summary of Part 3:

- An Accountability Culture has to be *created*. This takes time, money and long-term commitment, led from the top.
- It needs a positive, pro-active, cross-functional team—who agree on a Causal Model for how marketing and advertising effort affect business performance.
- The system must account for the "now and later" aspect of Accountability, and measure Brand Equity with great care.
- Metrics must be aligned with corporate objectives. They should also be limited in number. A typical upper limit is twenty, with "drill down" capability for other detail.
- Indiscriminate over-measurement can destroy creativity. Given the importance of creativity to business success, this Vulcan-Earthling issue needs to be handled sensitively.
- Often, the answer will be a Marketing Dashboard and Brand Scorecard. These "measure what matters for the people who matter" and give hard evidence of the Marketing and Advertising contribution to the success of the business.

### End of Part 3

This brings us to the end of *Vulcans, Earthlings and Marketing ROI*. The Useful Links that follow will help you chart your own path to a higher level of Marketing Accountability. Please note, however, that we are not endorsing any approach (or, by omission, de-endorsing others).

# Useful Links

## On Marketing Accountability:

www.marketingnpv.com
www.marketingprofs.com
www.zibs.com
www.ipa.co.uk
www.cassies.ca

Blogs:
www.customersandcapital.com
www.marketonomy.com

## Brand Valuation League Tables:

www.interbrand.com/surveys.asp
www.millwardbrown.com/Sites/Optimor/Content/KnowledgeCenter/
  BrandzRanking2007.aspx
www.brandfinance.com/docs/global_brands_survey.asp

## Practitioner Websites:

Canada:
www.custometrics.ca
www.kneebone.ca
www.venturecommunications.ca

US:
www.biz360.com
www.emmgroup.net
www.hudsonrivergroup.com
www.mma.com

# Glossary

The Austro-Hungarian Emperor Joseph II may never have said, "Too many notes, my dear Mozart," but there are certainly too many terms in our line of work. We thought a listing of the more common ones might be helpful.

Note that to avoid having to repeat "product, service or brand" on each occasion, we will just use "brand."

**Accountability Culture.** One of the aims of this book. A co-operative relationship within a company, and with its outside partners, based on getting the best available evidence on the efficacy of marketing and advertising effort—while not stifling innovation and creativity.

**Added Values.** A term used to describe the "moreness" that distinguishes a brand from the underlying functional product.

**Adoption Process.** The stages in adopting a brand—assumed to start with Awareness (but see Low Involvement Processing) and leading to Loyalty or Bonding to a greater or lesser degree. There are differing views as to how sequential the process is. See AIDA and Learn-Feel-Do.

**AIDA.** An acronym for Attention-Interest-Desire-Action, first proposed a hundred years ago as the sequential steps required for effective selling and advertising. AIDA seems sensible. Over the intervening years, however, experience has shown that it is not necessarily the right mechanism. See Hierarchy of Effects, Learn-Feel-Do, and Low Involvement Processing.

**Apollo.** See Project Apollo.

**Asset.** In the financial sense, a resource (tangible or intangible) with economic value, that offers the expectation of future cash flow. For accountants, assets are what are recorded on the left hand side of the Balance Sheet, which lists what the company owns. They are divided into current assets (expected to be consumed within a year, such as inventory) and fixed assets (those with a longer life, such as machinery and buildings). See Tangible and Intangible Assets.

**Attitude.** The negative or positive view that someone can have towards a company or brand (or its advertising). It may be based in Emotional and/or Rational responses. It is often measured as a guide to how well a brand is doing, though Attitudes do not always result in changes in Behaviour.

**Attributes.** Characteristics of a brand that are important to consumers. Sometimes used interchangeably with Features. Also linked to Benefits, though this can lead to finger-wagging debate over the question "Is it a feature or a benefit?" For example, Tide has a generous sudsing level. This is a feature. But is it also a benefit? In this case yes, because most people (though not all) equate high sudsing to cleaning performance. There's a general belief that it is better to establish benefits than features—though this seems to forget the need to be different. For example, in the early days of fluoride toothpastes Colgate and Crest both claimed to reduce cavities (a benefit). And both had fluoride (a feature). How did Crest differentiate itself? It got the endorsement of the American and Canadian Dental Associations first. Is this a feature or a benefit? Strictly speaking it's a feature. Though, as with Tide's sudsing, it's easy for consumers to see it as a benefit. As can be seen, these debates sometimes generate more heat than light. It does not especially matter if something is an attribute, a feature, or a benefit. What matters is how well it answers the consumer question "what's in it for me?" See also Values.[1]

**Audience (Target).** The people that a brand chooses to aim at. Audiences are often identified by demographics, but that is usually considered inadequate. They are also identified by usage e.g. users, non-users, occasional users etc., and attitudes. See Demographics and Psychographics.

**Awareness.** Measured for a brand, and/or its advertising, and subdivided into Unaided, Aided, Top of Mind and Total Awareness. It is generally assumed that high/growing awareness is good, but the "line of sight" between awareness and marketplace success is not linear. See also Low Involvement Processing and (Relevant) Differentiation.

**Balance Sheet.** One of three key financial statements of a business (along with the Income Statement and the Cash Flow Statement). It states the assets,

---

1 Crest also had the highly effective "Look Ma. No Cavities" campaign—reinforcing the point that advertising is often the big differentiator.

liabilities and shareholders' equity of the business at a point in time. It is called a Balance Sheet because, the assets of a company must equal the liabilities and equity of the company. The total of what the company owns (assets) is matched by what it has borrowed (liabilities) or raised from investors (equity).

**Balanced Scorecard.** See page 95.

**Baseline.** Used to define "the sales that we would have got in any event." Usually applies to sales or profits that would have accrued without marketing/advertising effort. Often associated with Marketing Mix Models.

**BCG Matrix.** The Boston Consulting Group process for classifying brands in terms of potential, with segments known as Stars, Dogs, Cash Cows and Question Marks. Stars, as the name suggests, deserve investment. For the others, investment is less likely, or actively withheld. This is intuitively appealing, though there has been some suggestion that the approach can miss opportunities, and become a self-fulfilling prophesy.

**Behaviour.** What people do, as opposed to what they *say* they do, or how they *feel.* Ultimately, it is only behaviour that turns attitudes and intentions into money for the brand owner.

**Benefit.** The characteristic(s) in a brand that make it desirable or, to use the economics term, that deliver Utility. Some people debate the difference between Attributes, Features and Benefits. So, it's an Attribute or Feature that a decaf coffee had no caffeine, but it's a Benefit that you aren't kept awake at night. Benefits can be based in reason or emotion or self-expression. Tide gets clothes clean, but it can also be trusted, and it makes you feel that you are doing a good job. See Attributes.

**Bonding.** A measure of how committed consumers are to a brand—measured in different ways by different research companies. It tries to assess how loyal consumers are, and in particular how inclined they are to stay with a brand despite inducements to go with another. See also Loyalty.

**Book Value.** The accounting value of a firm, calculated as the net of the liabilities and the assets on the Balance Sheet. Often called the "net asset value" for that reason. Theoretically, Book Value represents the liquidation value of a business i.e. the amount that the shareholders would receive if the company stopped doing business.

**Brand.** A brand—though we are surrounded by them—is hard to define with any precision. There is the legalistic or dictionary definition that focuses on the name, term, symbol or design that identifies a product. For our purposes, though, a brand is far more than this. It is the sum total of the perceptions and realities that make up what people think and believe about a product. See the definition on page 12.

**Brand Architecture.** The term used to describe how brands in a company can, or should, relate to each other. It covers stand-alone brands, and master brands. For example, Unilever uses Brand Architecture to help decide how to position its various detergents, and the many sub-brands that have the Lipton master brand name.

**Brand Associations.** Part of David Aaker's concept of Brand Equity, equating to "anything that connects the customer to the brand." The associations appear to be mostly in the mind, and in that sense are not unlike Ambler's "what we carry around in our heads about a brand."

**Brand Building.** The usual term for trying to create a profitable, growing, long-term asset, as opposed to milking a brand for short-term profit. Advertising, when done well, has a key role to play in brand building.

**Brand Equity.** Like many "brand" concepts, people use Brand Equity with different meanings, though they all include the idea that a brand is a valuable intangible asset. See Chapters 1.10 and 1.11 for definitions by Aaker and Ambler. See also Chapter 3.6 for how Brand Equity can act like a bridge between Brand Image and Brand Value.

**Brand Equity Models.** See Chapter 3.9.

**Brand Essence.** A concept popularized by David Aaker and others. The Brand Essence Statement can take various forms, but usually tries to compress what a brand stands for into a few inspiring words. Brand Essence Statements are for internal use only, and are not slogans or taglines. They can be extremely difficult to write, and run the risk of being what F. Ross Johnson—former CEO of RJR Nabisco—called a blinding glimpse of the obvious. Aaker gives two examples, and they reveal the difficulty. For Virgin, he has just one word—*iconoclasm*—and this marvellously captures Richard Branson's company. For IBM, he suggests *magic you can trust*. This does not resonate nearly as well. Aaker also points out that Brand Essence "is often ambiguous, especially when it is reduced to a few words or phrases." In other words, as a statement, it should not be expected to capture everything.

**(Total) Brand Experience.** This is a holistic way of thinking about how consumers interact with a brand. This was always the intention of the 4Ps, but over time, they have had a tendency to develop in the separate silos of product, packaging, sales promotion, advertising, etc. This is less than ideal, because consumers build up their impression of a brand from every point of contact—see later. (Note: this concept is also sometimes referred to as the Total Customer Experience.)

**Brand Health.** A general term for describing the condition of a brand—sometimes defined in very specific terms using metrics for relevance, differentiation, awareness, customer satisfaction etc.

**Brand Identity.** A term usually used for the graphic elements of a brand, though with a broader meaning by David Aaker. He uses it as "the set of associations that the brand strategist seeks to create and maintain," and his Brand Identity Planning Model embraces all brand-building activity. He also distinguishes Brand Identity from Brand Image, with Brand Image as the current set of associations, that may or may not be satisfactory. Brand Identity is the aspiration or goal.

**Brand Image.** Used by many to mean the collective set of impressions in the consumer's mind, and very close to what Aaker calls Brand Equity and what Ambler calls "what we carry around in our heads about a brand." We find it useful to separate Brand Image, Brand Equity and Brand Value, as mentioned in Chapter 3.6.

**Brand Loyalty.** See Loyalty.

**Brand Paradox.** The fact that brands are created by successful marketing effort, but do not usually come spiralling out of the sky if they are under-supported for a while. This creates the temptation to milk brands, rather than keep building them. See page 61.

**Brand Personality (or Brand Character).** People develop relationships with brands, and they attribute characteristics to them such as "trustworthy," "exciting," "past its prime" and so on. Marketing and Advertising establish and build the Brand Personality that will best serve the brand, bearing in mind what is achievable.

**Brand Reinforcement.** There is a tendency to see Marketing in terms of *change*. However, a great deal of brand success comes from *reinforcing* the impressions and associations that have been achieved, rather than trying to change them. Brand Reinforcement seeks to do this.

**Brand Resonance Model** (Kevin Lane Keller). See Chapter 3.9.

**Brand Value.** The financial worth of Brand Equity. It is calculated for different purposes and by different methods, and this will lead to a different figure. See Chapters 3.10 and 3.11.

**Brand Valuation.** The process—there are a number—for deriving the financial value of a brand. The two most credible methodologies are "relief from royalty" and "earnings split." The resulting brand valuations, though extremely important for specific purposes, are not precise enough for evaluating marketing or advertising activity. In other words, it would be misleading to calculate the Brand Value at the end of each fiscal year, and from that, and that alone, make conclusions about the efficacy (or not) of marketing effort.

**Brand Value Models.** See Chapters 3.10 and 3.11.

**BrandAsset® Valuator (BAV).** See Chapter 3.9.

**BrandDynamics.™** See Chapter 3.9.

**Cannibalization.** Sales gained by one brand at the expense of another in the company's portfolio.

**Cash Cow.** A brand that is being milked.

**Cash Flow.** A measure of the money coming into, and going out of, a company. Simplistically, it represents the difference between revenue and expenses— but note that it also includes any new financing raised or investments made.

Current cash flow is important, but sustained, healthy, *future* cash flow is critical for Shareholder Value.

**Cash Flow Statement.** One of the three key financial statements of a business (the others being the Income Statement and the Balance Sheet). It is generally produced every quarter and summarizes all the cash received from operating the business, plus any new financing raised, minus the operating costs of the business and any investments made.

**Causal Model.** See pages 10 and 74 and most of Part 3.

**Channels.** The distribution system. Note that a company can get a sustainable advantage here [for example, a better "just in time" system] and this can be a contributor to Brand Equity.

**Churn.** A metric for measuring customers lost—usually defined as a percent of the going-in base level—over a defined period e.g. a quarter or year.

**Commitment.** A metric—related to Bonding and Loyalty—for the probability of repeat purchase and usage.

**(Sustainable) Competitive Advantage.** A benefit or value that one brand "owns," and others are not able to match. At one time SCA was seen mostly as a tangible entity: a patented product advantage, or an exclusive manufacturing process, for example. Now, it has become clear that SCA can often come from intangibles, e.g., the *beliefs* that powerful brands build up in the minds of their audiences.

**Concept Testing.** A term used in product and advertising development. The objective of a concept test is to get a (hopefully reliable) indication of how a proposed idea resonates with consumers. There are debates about how best to do this. If the concept is too loosely described or illustrated, consumers can have trouble relating to it. But if it is highly finished consumers often react too much to the specifics. Advertisers, researchers and agencies have different views on this, and it is as well to make sure that everyone is aligned.

**Consumer.** The end-user who buys or uses a brand. Note that some companies are becoming self-conscious about the planet-damaging implication of the term "consumer." See also Customer.

**Core Brands.** The brands designated as essential to a business, and by extension the ones that get the most attention from top management.

**Core Values.** A term similar to Brand Essence, used by some to describe the essence of what a company or brand stand for.

**Corporate Identity.** Like Brand Identity, used by some to mean the graphic presentation of a company, but by others to encompass the entirety of how a company behaves and presents itself.

**Credibility.** A more difficult concept than it appears, because we are Earthlings, not Vulcans. To a Vulcan, something is credible or not according to logic and evidence. With Earthlings, it isn't necessarily so. As Jeremy Bullmore, a leading advertising figure in the UK said, "If I tell you that there are a million cats in the garden, I don't expect you to believe that there are a million, but I do expect you to believe that there are more than three." This points up that exaggeration or hyperbole, when properly done, can still be credible. See also Permission to Believe.

**Cross-Selling.** (Also Up-Selling.) Trying to get customers of a given product to buy one or more other products from the same company.

**Customer.** The general term for the clientele of a company, often used interchangeably with "Consumer." Note that sometimes "Customer" has a specific meaning. In B2B it means the immediate client, who may or may not be the end-user. In Packaged Goods, it means the retail trade. See also Consumer.

**Customer (Lifetime Value of).** An attempt to measure the net present value of a customer, i.e. the discounted value of the cash flow that they generate over the life of their relationship with the company.

**Customer Relationship Marketing.** Calling people at dinner time and asking them how they are, before trying to sell them something they don't want. Or, more seriously, effort taken to develop and manage relationships with customers over the long haul—embracing customer needs, customer service, complaint handling, telemarketing, e-marketing and similar "one on one" activities.

**Customer Utility Models.** See Chapter 3.8.

**Database Marketing.** Marketing effort driven by electronic information obtained from actual and potential customers, and stored in databases. The underlying idea is to know so much about a customer (while respecting privacy laws, etc.) that they can be marketed to in a customized "one on one" way.

**Demographics.** The statistical information that defines audiences, such as sex, age, income, education, family structure. See Psychographics.

**Depth Interview.** A long interview, almost always one-on-one though occasionally in pairs, between an expert and carefully chosen respondents. Because of time and expense, a brand almost never does enough interviews for statistical significance. Nevertheless, they can be a source of great insights and business-building ideas.

**Diagnostics.** Used to mean the information that *explains* Metrics, as opposed to the Metrics themselves.

**Difference (Point of).** An idea related to the concept of Unique Selling Proposition. Historically, it has been associated with product features and benefits, as in "Melts in your mouth; not in your hands" and "Dove. Won't dry your skin the way soap can." More generally, it applies to anything—including Emotional and Self-Expressive Benefits—that meaningfully separates a brand from its competitors. See the next entry.

**(Relevant) Differentiation.** A core concept in Brand Building. A brand must be relevant, but must also be seen as different (in a good way) from competitors. Relevant Differentiation may be rooted in Reality or Perceptions. It may trace to Rational benefits, or Emotional ones. And Emotional benefits may come from the brand (e.g. this is the one I trust) or self-image (e.g. this brand reflects well on me.) As a general rule, it is best if the difference can be expressed very succinctly, but it is not always that simple. For example, people have a strong sense that Nike is different from Reebok or Adidas, but it's hard to pin this down to a single point of difference. This leads to the Iceberg Challenge. Brands are complex, but they have to be presented simply. See Chapter 2.3.

**Direct (Response) Marketing.** Effort—mostly via mail, TV, radio, the internet, and the telephone—characterized by (a) a measurable response mechanism, (b) an offer or inducement to stimulate that response, and (c) the systematic use of data to identify target audiences and continuously hone effectiveness.

**Discounted Cash Flow (DCF).** The value of anticipated future cash flows expressed in today's dollars—this involves discounting the cash flows by an interest rate that reflects the Time Value of Money (see below) and an appropriate risk premium. DCF is a powerful tool for assessing the desirability of projects for which the cash inflows and outflows occur in different time periods.

**Distribution.** Logistically, the supply chain from manufacturer to retail outlet or end user. Also, the availability of product to consumers as in "we used to have 78% distribution, but now it stands at 85%." Distribution also involves the impression created by *where* a brand is bought. Some beauty products, for example, limit their distribution to upscale outlets, even though they could sell more—for a while at least—by expanding to the supermarket and the big box outlets. See also Channels.

**Earnings before Interest, Taxes, Depreciation and Amortization (EBITDA).** One of the key measures of a company's underlying profitability. It eliminates the effects of financing and accounting decisions to reveal the operating earnings the business.

**Earthlings.** See Chapter 1.7.

**Economic Value Added (EVA).** Another way of expressing financial performance, developed by Stern Stewart. It takes operating profit after taxes and deducts a charge for the capital used. The idea is to express the true economic profit of a company by measuring the extent to which the company has earned more than the Opportunity Cost (see below) of the capital it is using.

**Elasticity.** A ratio for how much one thing changes (e.g. sales) if something else changes (e.g. price or advertising spend level.) Sales would be inelastic if they changed very little, and elastic if they changed a lot. Elasticity, or the lack of it, may be good or bad e.g. if a brand holds sales despite a price increase, that would be good. But if sales do not respond to increased spending, that would be bad. Note that elasticity is sometimes used out of context. For example Marketing Mix Models will sometimes report on the "elasticity" of advertising, but usually do not point out that this is based on short-term measurement, missing the long-term effect. See Chapter 2.9.

**Emotional Benefits.** Academically, emotional benefits are impossible to define without sounding like a psychology textbook. At a more everyday level, we can think of them as the positive feeling we have towards a brand or ourselves as a result of marketing effort. As an example, many car brands tap into the joy of driving, and many packaged goods brands have a sub-text of "you are a good homemaker." See also Rational and Self-Expressive Benefits.

**End User.** The person (or animal) who consumes the product. This distinguishes the end user from intermediaries like the trade, or the purchaser.

**Enterprise Value.** The most complete value of a company. It represents what you would need to pay in order to acquire all the assets—buying out holders of all equity and debt. Enterprise Value is the sum of Market Capitalization (see below) and net debt (i.e. borrowing minus any cash).

**Equity.** One of the most problematic of terms because it is used in so many different contexts with specific—and different—meanings. In Finance it means ownership interest—the proportion of an asset that is owned once all borrowing is deducted. In Accounting, it is one of the three components of the Balance Sheet (along with assets and liabilities) and represents the money originally contributed by the owners plus the retained earnings of the business. In Marketing and Advertising it usually refers to the "moreness" that an Earthling perceives over what a Vulcan would judge to be the intrinsic value of a product or service.

**Equity*Builder.**™ See Chapter 3.9.

**Equity Engine.**™ See Chapter 3.9.

**Every Point of Contact.** The idea that people build up their impressions of brands from a whole host of sources. These include using the product, seeing it on the shelf, noticing the sort of people who use it, comments (good and bad) on the internet, marketing/advertising effort (to the extent that it gets seen), treatment by employees when contacting the company, the state of branded company trucks as they hurtle down the road, and so on. Marketing and Advertising people have to think about all of these when deciding the best way to get the brand story out.

**Fallacy of the Clean Slate.** Reference to the fact that marketers can (mistakenly) assume that the audience's mind is free and clear, when in fact it is almost always cluttered by preconceptions—often deeply held.

**Familiarity.** One of the concepts used in assessing Bonding. It is similar to awareness but implies something more than just knowing the name.

**(Price) Features.** A term commonly used in packaged goods, and usually associated with a special price, an in-store display, and often a mention in the retailer's flyer. Features have a dramatic effect on short-term sales, though, at least to some extent, they are subsidizing users who would have paid full price.

**Frequency.** A media term for the number of times an advertising message is delivered within a set period of time to the average target consumer. See also Reach.

**Functional Benefits.** Strictly speaking, the benefits of a brand that can be objectively measured or, in the language of this book, the benefits that a Vulcan would recognize.

**Generic Name.** In general marketing, a brand name that has lost all or most of its exclusivity e.g. zipper, aspirin, kleenex. In pharmaceutical marketing, the name of the molecule, as distinct from the patented brand name.

**Goodwill.** The difference between the purchase price of a business and its Book Value. Taken to represent the value of the intangible assets being acquired. See also Intangible Value and Chapter 1.13.

**Gross Rating Points (GRPs).** A measure of broadcast media weight, arithmetically equal to Reach times Frequency. In Tracking Studies, (in an attempt to exclude the effect of media weight) it is now common for the results to be reported for a given level of GRPs.

**Harvesting/Milking.** Extracting cash flow from a brand without reinvesting to build Brand Equity. See also Cash Cow.

**Hierarchy of Effects.** The notion that marketing and advertising activity affects people in a predictable sequence, with the idea that effective effort will successfully negotiate each of the steps. It is now largely agreed that the buying process is not this neat and tidy, but remnants of the thinking still remain. See AIDA, Learn-Feel-Do, and Low Involvement Processing.

**High Involvement Brands.** Those over which consumers take considerable time and trouble before they decide to buy. High involvement may be due to rational factors (high price, performance, value etc.) and/or emotional ones (fear of being wrong, self-image etc.).

**Human Capital.** One of two forms of intangible capital put forward by Leif Edvinsson, a pioneer in this area. He proposed that intangible capital comprised structural capital and human capital—structural capital being "what is left behind in the business when the human capital goes home at night." His classification is problematic, though, in that human capital is not the property of the company. His work has been superseded by the International Accounting Standards Board's classification of intangible assets based on five forms of intellectual property (see Chapter 1.13).

**Iceberg Challenge.** See Chapter 2.3.

**Immediacy Effect.** See Chapter 2.4.

**Income.** Used somewhat loosely, but generally understood by the context. Gross Income is all the money that comes into a company—usually in a defined period—and is the same as Revenue. Net Income is Revenue minus Expenses, and is the same as Profit.

**Income Statement.** One of the three key financial statements of a business (the others being the Balance Sheet and the Cash Flow Statement). It shows the financial performance of the business over a given period (generally quarterly and by year), with the reported profits for that period. For this reason, the Income Statement is also known as the Profit and Loss Statement.

**Intangible Asset.** (See Chapter 1.13.) Delightfully described by Leif Edvinsson as "the type of asset that does not hurt when you drop it on your foot." It is any asset not physical in nature, and includes all intellectual property that a company owns—such as patents, customer databases, trademarks, copyrights—and by extension brands.

**Intangible Value.** The difference between Market Value (see below) and Book Value (see above). It describes the difference between what investors think a company is worth (as observed in the stock market) and what the accounting statements show. The difference is vast. On average for the S&P 500, the Book Value represents only about a quarter of the Market Value. This reflects two factors: (1) Book Value shows the historical cost of assets that may have appreciated considerably, such as property; (2) internally-generated assets (such as inventions, databases, relationships and brands) are not recorded on the Balance Sheet, and are therefore excluded from Book Value.

**Integrated Marketing Communications.** IMC emerged from the realization that consumers build up impressions of a brand at "every point of contact," and that there should consequently be substantial consistency in how the brand is presented at these points. In the early days of IMC, the shorthand for this was "having the same look and feel." This has since been refined, because "look and feel" does not necessarily translate from one medium to another. Nowadays, the notions of "same organizing idea" and "same brand essence" are being used. The intention is to keep the brand coherent, while using each medium in the way that works best.

**Intermediate Metric.** It has proved difficult to link inputs (e.g., marketing spending) to ultimate consumer behaviour. This has created a need for intermediate metrics such as awareness, purchase intent, willingness to recommend etc. Although they do not provide an unbroken "line of sight" to the bottom line they are an important part of the Causal Model in Chapter 3.4.

**Key Driver.** A strategy tactic or factor that is regarded as crucial to a brand's market or financial success, and therefore one that should be part of any measurement system.

**Learn-Feel-Do.** There have been many attempts to explain how marketing and advertising work, using a Hierarchy of Effects. AIDA (see above) was one of the early examples. A later one, with roughly the same sequence, was Awareness, Knowledge, Liking, Preference, Conviction and Purchase. By the 1980s, it was becoming clear that the buying process is not this linear, and the thinking turned to the relationship between what people learn, what they feel and what they do. [Cognition, Affect and Conation in the language of the academic literature.]

Foote, Cone & Belding examined different buying scenarios, and summarized them as Learn-Feel-Do, Feel-Learn-Do, and Do-Feel-Learn. LFD is similar to AIDA, and applies to high-involvement purchases. FLD applies to categories like cosmetics and perfumes. DFL applies to low-involvement products where there is (presumed to be) not much risk attached to the purchase. This type of thinking is important, because it very much influences what will become the agreed Causal Model. (See Chapter 3.4.)

It has to be said, though, that the approach has never been validated. In addition, it can introduce problems of self-fulfilling prophecy. IBM lost $US15 billion or more in the early 90s, before turning around under the leadership of Lou Gerstner. IBM is unquestionably in the high-involvement category, yet "Solutions for a Small Planet" (the launch campaign for the turnaround) was not in the "learn" camp at all.[2] Clearnet in Canada is

---

2  Nuns chatter in an Eastern European language, with English subtitles. It's hard to imagine anything less high-tech, which was deliberate. IBM didn't have a "learn" problem. It had a "feel" problem. The campaign was intentionally disarming, to offset IBM's arrogant image.

similar. Purchases are clearly high-involvement. Yet the "Future is Friendly" campaign is far more "feel" than "learn."

**Liabilities.** The debts or obligations of a company. For accountants, these appear on the right hand side of the Balance Sheet. Current liabilities are debts that are due to be paid within a year (such as money owed to suppliers, taxes and overdrafts). Long-term liabilities are those due to be repaid over a longer period (such as bank loans and bonds).

**Life Cycle Theory.** The belief (which we do not share) that brands go through a cycle of birth, growth, maturity, decline and death. The theory is misguided because it does not distinguish between products and brands. Brands can be constantly refreshed, by product improvements, advertising, packaging changes and the like. With brand thinking, even the buggy whip could have survived. Let's suppose you make the leading buggy whip: Excalibur. In scenario one, the motorcar arrives. According to life cycle theory your days are numbered, and you quietly prepare for oblivion. In scenario two, however, you reject life cycle theory. You note that Excalibur is made of top quality leather. It is also carried in the hand, and riders brandish it with pride. Are there transferable values here? Yes indeed. You launch a top-of-the-line new product: Excalibur leather driving gloves. And later you expand into goggles and sunglasses. Excalibur becomes the prestige brand for the new, well-heeled automotive class. So the buggy whip dies, but Excalibur lives on.

**Long Term.** See Short Term and Long Term.

**Low Involvement Brands.** Those bought without much consideration, and frequently by habit. People in Marketing and Advertising often refer to low involvement as if it's a problem, but it is good for the bottom line if a brand can become a well-entrenched and habitual purchase.

**Low Involvement Processing** (now called Low Awareness Processing.) A provocative development in the notions of how marketing and advertising work. The roots are in neuroscience, where it is known that our brains—at the lower or limbic level—take in huge amounts of information with no conscious knowledge that this is happening. Robert Heath and others have developed this into the proposition that advertising can be effective with low or even no conscious awareness. Given that awareness takes centre stage in most models of effective advertising, this is creating quite a stir. The theory resonates with some, in that we can relate to having thoughts or feelings about brands with no conscious recollection of where they came from. It's a complicated issue, and does not yet seem to have reached the mainstream. For more, see Heath R. in the References.

**Loyalty.** The degree to which consumers keep buying a given brand over time. In reality, brands have few *totally* loyal consumers, but the goal is to have as many as possible, as loyal a possible. This is a simple idea, but it is complicated by the difference between *attitudinal* and *behavioural* loyalty. Consumers may say "I always buy X" but actually have a repertoire of brands. Or they may be attitudinally disloyal ("I am unhappy with my bank") but stay anyway. Or they may be conditionally loyal e.g. favouring a given brand because of a loyalty programme, though not necessarily with any deep-seated sense of commitment to the brand.

**Loyalty Programme.** A marketing programme designed to retain customers by rewarding them for their continuing business.

**Marcom.** The abbreviation for marketing communication.

**Market Capitalization.** The total value of a company from the shareholder perspective (calculated by multiplying the number of shares by the current market price of one share). Frequently called Market Value (see next entry). Note that both terms are frequently confused with Enterprise Value (see above) that represents the overall value of the company, defined as Market Value plus net borrowing.

**Market Value.** Used by many websites/commentators as a synonym for Market Capitalization (see above). Note that Market Value only represents the proportion of the value of the business that is owned by the shareholders.

**Marketing Mix Models.** See page 82 and Chapter 2.9.

**Marketing Mix.** See Chapter 2.2.

**Measurability Effect.** See Chapter 2.4.

**Media Mix Models.** Models that use generalized and (where possible) brand specific databases to predict the media outcomes of various media mixes. A typical model, for a given budget, will examine various combinations of media, and predict a likely range for an important intermediate variable, e.g. brand or advertising awareness. These models help make difficult decisions as to how much effort any given medium should get, and still be above "threshold" levels. It has to be noted, of course, that these models are based on assumptions as to how the various media work, alone and in combination, and the field is still developing as more information is collected.

**Metrics.** A term used loosely to mean "things that we measure" but also with a more specific meaning from Tim Ambler, namely "quantified marketing performance measures regularly reviewed by top management." This is distinct from Diagnostics, which are "lower level measures that explain variances in metrics."

**"Moreness."** A term used to describe the totality of added values that distinguish a brand from the underlying functional product.

**Net Present Value (NPV).** The present value of future cash inflows and outflows, using Discounted Cash Flow (see above). Used to express the overall profitability of a strategy where cash flows occur over time (typically involving an initial investment period with cash outflows, followed by a period of cash inflows once the product or service gains traction in the market).

**Net Promoter Score.** See Willingness to Recommend.

**Opportunity Cost.** The cost of giving up one course of action to pursue another. Used in finance to assess the desirability of an investment by considering how the money might otherwise be used.

**Payment by Results.** Agency remuneration linked to achieving objectives. These vary, but are generally tied to some or all of (a) brand performance in market, (b) intermediate measures such as awareness or intent to purchase or brand health, (c) client service.

**Perceptual Maps.** See Chapter 3.8.

**Permission to Believe.** In many Creative Strategy or Briefing documents there is a "Support" or "Reason Why" section. This contains the evidence intended to make the main selling point convincing. When this line of thinking first developed, support statements almost always focused on a concrete reason why as in "X is the answer to your prayers because it contains Y magic ingredient." Over time, people started to realize that this approach was restrictive, and that the evidence in support of a brand could be more subtle. Out of this came the idea of "permission to believe." This is not necessarily the logical and provable evidence that would convince a Vulcan, but nevertheless it has persuasive power with Earthlings. See also Credibility.

**Positioning.** See Chapter 2.2.

**Product.** In this book it is reserved for the physical functional entity as in "A product is made in the factory. A brand is made in the mind." Note also that where we say "product" we also mean this to include services.

**Product Placement.** Having a brand used in movies, shows, etc., so as to create favourable and apparently "unadvertised" associations.

**Project Apollo.** A major single-source pilot test, looking to relate consumer buying to media exposure. It is led by Procter & Gamble, along with Unilever, SC Johnson, three companies who prefer not to be named, and the corresponding advertising agencies. Arbitron and ACNielsen have recruited 5,400 US panellists. Portable People Meters monitor their media exposure, and handheld scanners track their retail purchases. Early findings were presented June 2006 to delegates at the ESOMAR World Research Conference in Shanghai, China. Results suggest that mass media can effectively identify and influence brand loyalists and switchers. Arbitron eventually aims to recruit 30,000 panelists and hopes other marketers will be sufficiently intrigued to join the project and fund the expansion. [Entry derived from the *World Advertising Research Centre*.]

**Profit.** The same as Net Income—total earnings or revenue less expenses.

**Psychographics.** Characteristics used to identify consumer segments based on their lifestyle, personality, beliefs etc. See also Demographics.

**Pull and Push.** Pull relies on creating demand from the end user, e.g. through advertising. Push implies loading the wholesaler or retailer, thereby exerting pressure for onward sales.

**Purchase Intent.** A measure of a buyer's claimed likelihood of purchasing a brand next time or sometime in the future. There are technical difficulties related to claimed intent versus actual behaviour, but the major research companies have developed methodologies that are sufficiently robust to deal with this for brand management purposes.

**Qualitative and Quantitative Research.** Qualitative Research, such as focus groups and one-on-one interviews, probes respondents for thoughts, feelings, reactions, ideas etc. It does not project what will happen in the population at large. All qualitative research reports are at pains to say this, but the results are frequently misused anyway. Quantitative Research, properly designed, does project what can be expected from the larger population—but it suffers from a different problem. If the design is poor, or questions are not asked in the right way, answers will likely give the wrong picture. Research is a frequent source of friction between Clients, Agencies and Research Houses. For more, see *Excellence in Brand Communication,* published by the ICA.

**Quality (Actual and Perceived).** Actual quality is measured objectively, and in the language of this book is what a Vulcan can see. Perceived Quality is in the eye of the beholder, who in our case is an Earthling. It is usually measured as Relative Perceived Quality in comparison to one or more other brands. The difference between actual and perceived quality is, for the most part, caused by the added values of the brand. In everyday life, consumers rarely have objective measures of quality, and in that sense quality is more or less always perceived. Relative Perceived Quality is closely correlated with Brand Equity and ROI. See Chapter 2.7.

Note: When products are functionally similar, superior marketing and advertising can and do improve Perceived Quality. However, it is a dangerous misconception to suppose that marketing and advertising can, over the long term, cover up for an inferior product.

**Rational Benefits.** Benefits that would appeal to a Vulcan, or to the left brain of an Earthling. See also Emotional and Self-Expressive Benefits.

**Reach.** A media term for the percentage of the target market who have the opportunity to see any advertisement in a campaign. See also Frequency.

**Reality and Perception.** See pages 11–12. Brands are a combination of reality and perception, in the sense that what lodges in our mind is influenced by the "objective reality" of a product, and the other meanings that we, as Earthlings, attribute to a brand.

**Recall.** A way to measure if an advertisement is cutting through. Unaided recall typically comes from a question like, "Can you remember any advertisements for financial services?" followed by questions to ascertain that the recall is attributed to the right brand. Aided recall names the brand as in, "Can you remember any ads for Scotiabank?" There are controversies about the validity of recall. The fact that we can recall something does not necessarily mean that we are persuaded by it. And the fact that we can't, at a given moment, recall something does not mean that it is not deeper in our minds. There are also disputes between research suppliers, whose techniques rely on recall to a greater or lesser degree. See also Recognition.

**Recognition.** Similar to recall, but based on different theories about memory. In recognition studies, respondents are shown advertisements, and asked if they recognize them. There is academic evidence to say that this is more reliable than recall for finding if an advertisement has broken through. However, recognition questions have a placebo effect i.e. people may say they recognize something when they have never seen it before. A good study needs to control for this.

**Relative Price.** An important Brand Equity metric. A brand's average selling price relative to competitors, taking list price and promotional discounting into account.

**Relevance.** See (Relevant) Differentiation.

**Revenue.** The top line or gross income received during a given period.

**ROI.** Return on Investment. Technically defined as funds generated minus funds invested, divided by funds invested. Often misused by Marketing and Advertising as a catch-all term for Accountability. See Chapter 1.1.

**Self-Expressive Benefits.** Some people distinguish between Emotional Benefits and Self-Expressive Benefits, though others treat them under one heading. To Aaker, Emotional Benefits have their roots in product as in "I like the safety I feel with Volvo." Self-Expressive Benefits link to self-image as in "Stella Artois makes a statement about me." See also Rational and Emotional Benefits.

**Shareholder Value.** A management concept that focuses decision-making on steadily increasing a company's value for shareholders—with the goal of a steadily improving stock price over the long term.

**Short Term and Long Term.** In this book, "short term" and "long term" have various meanings according to the context. In general, "short term" means "within the current fiscal year" or "within 12–18 months or so." By extension, "long term" usually means "beyond the current fiscal year" or "a year or more into the future" or on occasion "well out into the future."

**Six Sigma.** One of the Total Quality Management processes, apparently patented by Motorola, but now referred to generically. It is a measure of the defect rate of any process.

**Tangible Asset.** A physical asset such as property, plant and equipment. Also includes cash, work in progress and inventory. Contrasts with intangible assets that are non-physical and generally involve intellectual property of some sort. See Intangible Assets.

**Target Market.** See Audience.

**Time Value (of Money).** A finance person's way of saying that a bird in the hand is worth two in the bush i.e. that a dollar today is worth more than a dollar tomorrow. There are two factors: (1) the certainty of receiving the money; and (2) the opportunity cost of the money.

**Top-of-Mind.** The degree to which a given brand is mentioned first when respondents are asked if they can recall a brand. Sometimes called "first mention." Can also be used with advertising.

**Total Customer Experience** See Brand Experience.

**Total Quality Management (TQM).** A process—some regard it as a philosophy—for making a company eat, live and breathe quality. It is largely credited to the work of W. Edwards Deming in Japan after World War II (and later in the US), though Armand V. Feigenbaum was developing similar ideas for General Electric at the same time.

**Utility.** See Chapter 1.12.

**Values.** (Not to be confused with Added Values.) In line with Maslow's Hierarchy of Needs, there is a general notion that Values are of a higher order than Benefits and Features, though they are all related to how consumers develop preferences for one brand over another. Consider an Orange Juice without pulp (a Feature) that is a pleasure to drink (a Benefit) and also makes you feel like a great homemaker (a Value). As this example shows, Features, Benefits and Values overlap with Rational and Emotional Benefits, and this can get tricky, especially when the debate turns to keeping a message single-minded. In addition, it is usually difficult for a brand to rely on a product-based reason when it tries to "own" something at the Values end of the spectrum. This is not to say that a brand can't own a Value—many of the major brands do—but the reason why (to the degree that there is one) usually draws heavily on emotional responses.

**Vulcans and Earthlings.** See Chapter 1.7.

**Vulcan–Earthling Dissonance.** The differences of opinion between those who take a pure "logic and reason" approach to business, and those who believe that Earthling consumers use and buy many brands for any number of emotional and non-rational reasons that a Vulcan simply does not understand.

**Wear-In.** The notion that some types of advertising need time—several exposures—before they become effective. Note that this view, and the following one for wear-out, are the source of some debate and disagreement.

**Wear-Out.** The notion that individual advertisements, though usually not the overall campaign, lose their effectiveness after repeated exposure. Wear-out makes intuitive sense, and most practitioners seem to believe in it. It has to noted, though, that there are various examples, particularly in the past, of successful business-building ads that ran virtually unchanged for years.

**Willingness to Recommend.** A surrogate for the strength of Brand Equity, and one of the variables that this book recommends as a metric. This idea has been popularized by Fred Reichheld using the concept of a Net Promoter Score (the net of the proportion of your customers who are willing to recommend your brand minus the proportion unwilling to do so).

**Winning B®ands.** See Chapter 3.9.

# References

Aaker, D.A. (2004) *Brand Portfolio Strategy*. The Free Press.
—— and Joachimstaler, E. (2000) *Brand Leadership*. The Free Press.
—— and Jacobson, R. (1994) "The Financial Information Content of Perceived Quality." *Journal of Marketing Research*.
Ambler, T. (2004) "ROI Is Dead: Now Bury It." *Admap*, September.
——. (2003) *Marketing and the Bottom Line*. FT Prentice Hall.
Association of National Advertisers. (2004) *Survey of 54 ANA Members*. July.
Baxter, M. (1999) "Advertising and Profitability: The Long-Term Returns." *Admap*. July.
Bedbury, S. (2002) *A New Brand World*. Viking.
Bergesen, M. and Ehrbar A. (2002) "A New Approach to Managing Brand and Business Value." *Institutional Investor Journals*. November.
Biel, A. (1990) "Marketing Accountability: Strong Brand, High Spend." *Admap*. November.
Blair, M.H. and Rosenberg, K.E. (1994) "Convergent Findings Increase Our Understanding of How Advertising Works." *Journal of Advertising Research*. May/June. [See also Lodish]
Broadbent, S. (2001) "If the Question Is Ad Effects the Answer Is Not Elasticities." *Journal of Advertising Research*. March/April.
——. (1997) *Accountable Advertising*. ISBA/IPA/Admap Publications.
Buck, S. (2002) *The True Cost of Cutting Adspend*. World Advertising Research Centre.
Butterfield, L. [Editor] (2003) *AdValue*. IPA/Butterworth Heinemann.
Buzzel, R. and Gale, B. (1987) *The PIMS Principles*. The Free Press.
Cassies. Canadian Advertising Success Stories. www.cassies.ca.
Cioffi, J. and Miller, A. (2004) "The Unisys Marketing Dashboard." *Journal of Advertising Research*. September.
Doyle, P. (2000) *Value Based Marketing*. John Wiley & Sons.
Duffy, M. (2002) "Measuring Marketing ROI. Great but Usually Late." *MSI Conference*. #02-119.
EMM Group. (2004) *The New Marketing Mission*. Association of National Advertisers.
Feldwick, P. (1997) "Agency, Client and Researcher: The Eternal Triangle." *Admap*. June.
——. (1998) "A Brief Guided Tour through the Copy-Testing Jungle." *Admap*. January.

Fortini-Campbell, L. (1992) *Hitting the Sweet Spot.* Copy Workshop.

Haigh, D. and Knowles, J. (2004) *Measuring and Valuing Brand Equity.* ICA–Institute of Communication Agencies.

Heath, R. (2001) "Low Involvement Processing—A New Model of Brand Communication." *Journal of Marketing Communications.* March.

Hess, M. and Ambach, G. (2002) *Short and Long Term Effects of Advertising and Promotion.* American Association of Advertising Agencies.

IPA: *Advertising Works* (Winning cases from the IPA Effectiveness Awards). World Advertising Research Centre.

Jadidi, K., Mela, C. F. and Gupta, S. (1998) "Managing Advertising and Promotion for Long-Term Profitability." Marketing Science Institute.

Jones, J. P. (1995) *When Ads Work: New Proof that Advertising Triggers Sales.* Lexington Books. [See also Lodish]

———. (1986) *What's in a Name.* Lexington Books.

Kaplan, R. S. and Norton, D. P. (1996) *The Balanced Scorecard.* Harvard Business School Press.

Keller, K. L. (2000) "Brand Report Card." *Harvard Business Review.* January/February.

Knowles, J. (2003) "Learning to Like Each Other." *Professional Investor.* February.

———. (2004) "Putting a Value on Your Branding Activities." *AMA Better Marketing ROI with Marketing Dashboards Conference.* New York. November.

——— and Ettenson, R. (2007) "Reconcilable Differences." *Harvard Business Review.* June.

LaPointe, P. (2005) *Marketing by the Dashboard Light.* Association of National Advertisers.

Lenskold, J. D. (2003) *Marketing ROI.* AMA/McGraw Hill.

Lodish, L. M. (1997) "J. P. Jones and M. H. Blair on Measuring Advertising Effects—Another Point of View." *Journal of Advertising Research.* September/October.

——— and Lubetkin, B. (1992) "General Truths? Nine Key Findings from the IRI Test Data." *Admap.* November.

Madden, T. J., Fehle, F. and Fournier, S. (2006) "Brands Matter: An Empirical Demonstration of the Creation of Shareholder Value through Branding." *Journal of the Academy of Marketing Science.* April.

McDonald, C. "Is Your Advertising Working?" *Admap Monograph #9.* World Advertising Research Centre.

———. (1997) *Monitoring Advertising Performance.* Admap/NTC Publications.

Middleton, A. C. (2005) *Measuring Marketing Communication Returns.* ACA–Association of Canadian Advertisers.

Mizik, N. and Jacobson, R. (2005) "How Brand Attributes Drive Financial Performance." *Marketing Science Institute.*

Pauwels, K., Silva-Risso, J., Srinivasan, S. and Hanssens, D. (2004) "New Products, Sales Promotions, & Firm Value: The Case of the Automobile Industry." *Journal of Marketing.* October.

Percy, L. (1997) *Strategies for Implementing Integrated Marketing Communications.* NTC Business Books.

Reichheld, F. (1996) *The Loyalty Effect.* Harvard Business School Press.

———. (2001) *Loyalty Rules!* Harvard Business School Press.

Rust, R.T., Ambler, T., Carpenter, G., Kumar, V. and Srivastava, R. K. (2004) "Measuring Marketing Productivity." *Journal of Marketing.* October.

Rutherford, D. [Editor] (2003) *Excellence in Brand Communication.* ICA—Institute of Communication Agencies.

Schultz, D. E. and Walters, J. S. (1997) *Measuring Brand Communications ROI.* Association of National Advertisers.

Srivastava, R. K., Shervani, T. and Fahey, L. (1998) "Market-Based Assets and Shareholder Value." *Journal of Marketing.*

Steel, J. (1998) *Truth, Lies & Advertising: The Art of Account Planning.* Wiley.

# Diagram Sources

**Figure 1.8 - 1. A Brand Is More Than the Product or Service**
Adapted from *Excellence in Brand Communication*, published by the ICA
Rutherford D. [Editor] (2003)

**Table 1.9 - 1. Coke versus Pepsi (Blind and Identified Testing)**
Source: De Chernatony and Knox
From *Brand Vision to Brand Evaluation* (1990)

**Table 1.9 - 2. Brand Value Rankings by Interbrand and Millward Brown**
http://www.interbrand.com/best_brands_2007.asp
https://www.millwardbrown.com/Sites/Optimor/Content/
    KnowledgeCenter/BrandzRanking2007.aspx

**Figure 1.9 - 3. The Performance of Strongly Branded Companies**
Source: Madden, Fehle and Fournier (2006)
http://www.hbs.edu/research/facpubs/workingpapers/papers2/0102/
    02-098.pdf

**Figure 1.13 - 1. The Growth of Intangible Assets**
Source: S&P 500 – Market-to-Book Ratio (Dec. 1982 - Dec. 2006)
Analysis by Type 2 Consulting Inc
www.type2consulting.com

**Figure 2.7 - 1. Relative Ad Spend vs. Relative Perceived Quality**
Source: PIMS Europe Database (1998)

**Figure 2.7 - 2. Relative Ad Spend vs. Relative Image/Reputation**
Source: PIMS Europe Database (1998)

**Figure 2.7 - 3. Relative Customer Value and ROI**
Source: PIMS Europe Database (1998)

**Table 2.8 - 1. Test vs. Control Volume Growth**
Source: Lodish L. M., Lubetkin B. *General Truths? Nine Key Findings from the
IRI Test Data*. Admap. (November 1992)

**Figure 2.9 - 1 and 2. Marketing Mix Model Results Reported by Hess and Ambach**
Source: Hess M. and Ambach G. *Short and Long Term Effects of Advertising and Promotion.* American Association of Advertising Agencies. (2002)

**Table 2.10 - 2. Average Share Structure amongst Branded Goods**
Source: Buck S. *The True Cost of Cutting Adspend.* World Advertising Research Centre. (2002)

**Table 2.10 - 3. Changes in Average Adspend for Long-Term Winners and Losers**
Source: Buck S. *The True Cost of Cutting Adspend.* World Advertising Research Centre. (2002)

**Table 2.10 - 4. Average Share Structure amongst Branded Goods**
Source: Buck S. *The True Cost of Cutting Adspend.* World Advertising Research Centre. (2002)

**Figure 2.10 - 5. Winners vs. Losers (1997–2001)**
Source: Buck S. *The True Cost of Cutting Adspend.* World Advertising Research Centre. (2002)

**Figure 3.9 - 1. Equity Engine™**
Source: Research International
http://www.marketingclub.at/Veranstaltungen/rueckblick/
  viennaoct02_gesamt.pdf

**Figure 3 .9 - 2. BrandAsset® Valuator**
Source: Young & Rubicam
http://www.yrbav.com/

**Figure 3.9 - 3. Equity*Builder™**
Source: Ipsos Group
http://www.ipsos-asi.com/products/EquityBuilder.aspx

**Figure 3.9 - 4. BrandDynamics™**
Source: BrandZ/WPP
http://63.99.161.62/brandz/z3_what_21.html

**Figure 3.9 - 5. Brand Resonance Model**
Source: Kevin Lane Keller
http://smib.vuw.ac.nz:8081/WWW/ANZMAC2004/CDsite/papers/
Kuhn2.PDF

**Figure 3.9 - 6. Winning B®ands**
Source: AC Nielsen
http://www2.acnielsen.com/pubs/2003_q2_ap_winningbrands.shtml

**Figure 3.12 - 1. The Balanced Scorecard**
Adapted from Kaplan and Norton
http://www.balancedscorecard.org/basics/bsc1.html

**Figure 3.12 - 2. The Hilton Dashboard**
Source: MarketingNPV
http://www.marketingnpv.com/articles/features/Hilton_Drives_Premium_
Marketing_Performance_from_Balanced_Scorecard

# Index

# Easy Reference Card—The Value of Marketing*

| | Not Just ... | But Also ... |
|---|---|---|
| Objectives | Create customer value. | Use customer value to deliver Shareholder Value. |
| Strategy | Increase market share. | Develop and manage marketing assets. |
| Assumptions | Positive market performance leads to positive financial performance. | Marketing strategies need to be tested in value terms. Use of scenarios. Opportunity cost analysis. |
| Contribution | Knowledge of customers, competitors & channels. | Knowledge of how to use marketing to increase Shareholder Value. |
| Focus | Marketing orientation. | General management. |
| Advocacy | Importance of understanding customers. | Marketing's role in using Customer Value to create Shareholder Value. |
| Concept assets | Tangible. | Market based (often called intangibles). |
| Rationale | Improves profits. | Increases Shareholder Value. |
| Relationship with the board | Sales & margins. | Joint agreement on the format & presentation of marketing metrics. |
| Relationship with the strategy group | Coexistence. | Integration of business and marketing strategies. |
| Relationship with Finance | Different perspectives and language. | Agreement on key metrics and how to report them. |
| Performance metrics | Market share, customer satisfaction, return on sales and investment. | Shareholder Value via discounted cash flows, to link marketing inputs with financial outputs. |

---

\* Extracted from "What Value Marketing," a 2004 position paper by the Australian Marketing Institute. The table is based on the 2000 book by Peter Doyle, Value Based Marketing, published by Wiley.